ASA SMOUSE

ONE-OF-A-KIND

Survival guide for invisible scars

Prowess Publishers

First published by Prowess Publishers 2023

ONE-OF-A-KIND is available on Takealot.com, Amazon, Apple Books, and Kobo. You can also order directly from Asa Smouse through the following ways: 1) email: asa@asasmouse.com 2) website: www.asasmouse.com 3) call or WhatsApp: + 27 (0) 62-297-1312.

This memoir is based on uncensored truth. It reflects the author's present recollections of her experiences. No names have been changed, no characters manufactured and no events invented. Some dialogues have been paraphrased while taking care not to lose the essence of truth. Bible scriptures are taken from NKJV, NIV, AMPC, TPT and GNT.

Second edition

ISBN: 9780620939546

Advisor: Ree Smouse
Editing by Alan Barnard
Proofreading by Ntsikelelo Nqoyo
Cover art by Vassilis Antonakos

This book was professionally typeset on Reedsy.
Find out more at reedsy.com

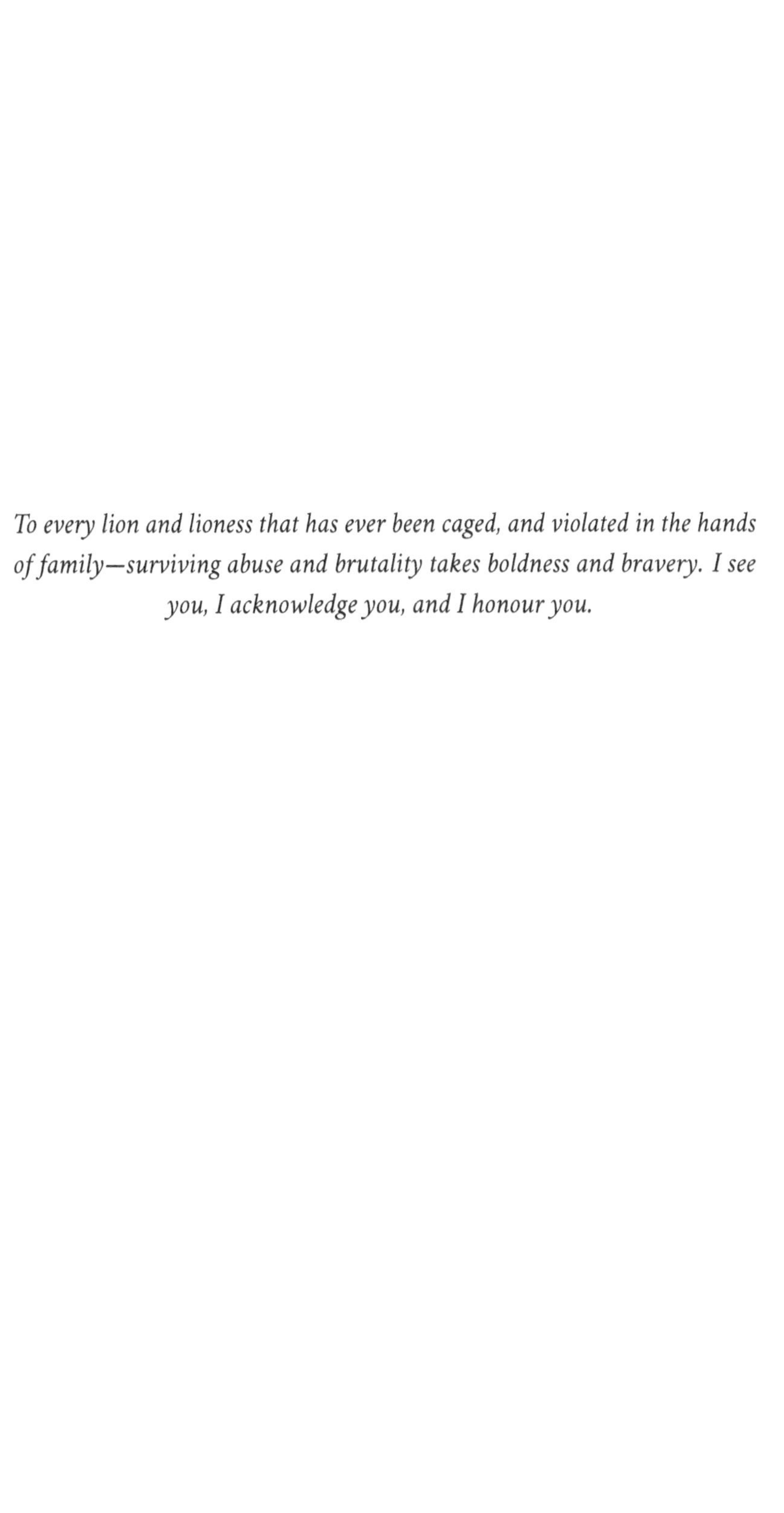

To every lion and lioness that has ever been caged, and violated in the hands of family—surviving abuse and brutality takes boldness and bravery. I see you, I acknowledge you, and I honour you.

"There are all these moments you think
you won't survive. And then you survive."

DAVID LEVITHAN

Contents

Preface

I once read whatever calamity you go through in life is not just for you, one day it will become someone else's survival guide. I've decided to write this as a survival guide for those that have either been through similar experiences like mine or are still battling with triggers from their childhood or past traumas. Either way, whatever unfinished business you may have, may you find the answers to your million unanswered questions in this survival guide. I pray that this book goes further than I can imagine, helps more people than I will ever meet, and heals more souls than I will ever know. May this survival guide give you the courage to step off the ledge and see the wings that you've always had, wings that you will need when your back is against the wall. If I could make it out of my hell alive when walls were closing in on me, I have no doubt that you too, can overcome.

It's funny how we have to be pushed out of our comfort zones before we get to realize how magnificent we are, each of us in our unique way. How we never know how strong we truly are until being strong becomes the default option.

This is me confessing that despite how courageous and confident I may be, I have been constantly bullied by what I've discovered to be the worst bully of all: the imposter syndrome. I tried fighting back so many times, telling myself that I am good enough, that I can write this guide. Guess what? I was defeated before I even began. The more I kept postponing sharing my story, making up all sorts of wonderful excuses, the more I had this nagging feeling that I needed to let it out.

Me being me, I pushed back and silenced the nagging feeling—or at least that's what I thought I was doing—until tragedy struck.

I bumped into this young man by pure chance. I had always known of his existence but never paid any attention to him. As I formally introduced myself to him we ended up talking about my childhood. A childhood that he could well resonate with.

From there he got to open up about his painful past, a past that for two decades he refused to talk about. He had been labelled a deep and arrogant child by family members—something that sounded familiar to me. He was also an extroverted introvert—an ambivert as the Ivy League call it.

On the day we met, I impetuously found myself as his unpaid therapist. I could see beyond his tough exterior, beyond the body builder's cape. Given insight into the window of his soul, I saw a little boy hopelessly screaming for help. He was drowning and was well aware of it. He wasn't prepared to ask for professional help, he didn't trust anyone, he told me he was not about to trust a system that failed him as a young boy, a system that does not possess the discernment required in a world full of abusive parents who hide so well behind the Bible.

He had not been well for some time, but in a way he could not explain. No doctor could help when he was taken to hospital, in the end, he was referred to a psychologist. It seemed like something was eating him up from the inside but no one could say what it was. There was anger there, effectively contained, but anger nevertheless. And I wonder today if it was not anger on top of a whole lot of unresolved feelings from his childhood that killed him. They did diagnose psychosomatic-related illnesses after all.

Would you blame a little boy sent to a Christian school proclaiming to be the best at modelling the love of Jesus for being angry when hostel staff glued his empty stomach to a wall because he asked for food?

Or having his head banged against a telephone booth for wanting to call his mother? Or having a father that would beat him and his older brother for playing around the house? A father who took pride in being a well-respected community figure?

I vividly remember the hardened edge of suppressed rage in his eyes and the black feeling he carried with him like a cloud. Polite to the end, humble, yet beneath the placid exterior, a thunderstorm was brewing.

I took what opportunity I had at that moment to relay some of my childhood experiences and it helped. I don't know if he ever got to talk to somebody like me or get the chance to hear something different to what he had heard before but suddenly he saw the world differently, he saw women differently. The chauvinist in him had believed that girls are weak and have it easy, that only boys had it hard.

He was suddenly calm and wanted to know how come I overcame my demons without killing my Goliath. He wanted to know the secret behind dreaming freely without being confined to the prison of your past.

He had taken a break from his studies and wanted to know. He was an exceptional student but his unattended trauma was starting to catch up with him—something I was very familiar with. It was his explicit cry for help that catapulted us into an emergency coaching session.

We agreed to meet up again in January but you know how it goes over the festive season. It was on a Sunday afternoon when I had a nagging feeling about scheduling a proper "catch-up" session with him.

The following morning I called, only to hear the tragic news that made me wish I had superpowers to turn back time. He was no more, found dead in his room the evening before.

My tears flowed uncontrollably when the surviving brother told me about the impression I had made on this young man. He had found someone he could trust, he said, someone who was speaking his language—a language barely spoken in a world of family that can be so pretentious and treacherous (his words). As much as I felt like I failed him and for days afterwards I was swamped with feelings of guilt and regret, it was a comfort to think I was able to reach him where he was at that moment.

Yes! A young man in his early twenties, a bright future ahead of him, had to die for me to be propelled to write this survival guide. He died before my eyes and I couldn't help but wonder if the outcome would have been different if I had managed to share a bit more with him. This is what I would have loved to tell him…

Acknowledgement

Firstly, I'd like to give all the glory to Jehovah God, the Holy One of Israel, the Great One in battle, for every mountain I have climbed and every valley He has seen me through. Please join me in exalting the One who answers by fire, who commands the winds and the seas—and they obey Him. Indeed, the seed of Jacob never sought the God of Jacob in vain. My sincere gratitude and appreciation go to my greatest crush, Ree for being incredibly supportive every step of the way and staying up all night just to keep me company while I talk to myself. Thank you for not getting tired of giving me advice even when I don't get to use it. Thank you for always being my number one cheerleader, not out of obligation, but out of the goodness of your heart. Above all, credit should be given to you my babe for respecting my decision to tell my story to the world at the cost of igniting your wounds, wounds you never realized were there, to begin with. Thank you to our four cubs: Amo, Khumo, Kamo, and JR who were so understanding as young as they are, they made room for my privacy during the writing process. Al, your invaluable contribution has fuelled me to dig deeper within my soul and propelled me to the finish line. It wasn't always easy to trust your recommendations as an editor. Thank you for pouring yourself into this project, and treating it with utter respect and the utmost sensitivity it required. Ntsikelelo and Rochelle, there wouldn't be this final product without you.

I

Part One

Innocence turned into filth

1

Built-in power

I t was in my middle school years when I was introduced to child slavery by the man who called himself my father. He had this brick manufacturing business that turned into an obsession. Allow me to introduce you to my first experience of work-life, at age 11. The first stage entailed sifting the soil in stages and spreading it onto the levelled ground. From there it was thoroughly broken down, watered, and kneaded.

I recall watching the workers packing the clay with their bare hands then pressing it into the moulds so it filled all the corners. I could see how passionate they were about their craft as they removed the extra clay, gently lifting the mould to reveal the raw brick—the beginning of my nightmare world.

Little did I know that the fascination I had with the production process of bricks—teaching me the importance of precision, stamina, excellence, attention to detail, and craftsmanship—ended up being the very curse that would turn my world upside down and turn me into a slave in my home-turned-prison.

Drying is one of the most important steps in the brick-making process for one simple reason: to avoid cracks. If and when damp bricks are mistakenly taken directly for burning it will result in cracking which then means wastage and loss of time and money along the production line. Over time I learned that the drying time affected the overall strength of the raw bricks, enabling them to be stacked to greater heights for firing. In all this, I don't recall once applying to be the errand girl that soon had a daily routine after school—expected to show up at work with no excuses of homework or afternoon classes when I reached high school. What I can tell you is how I got recruited. It was one evening during the week when I opened the refrigerator in our kitchen intending to get an apple.

Yip, it all started with an apple. I accidentally broke one of the glass shelves in the process of manoeuvring my way around the shelves stuffed with pots and plates to get to the apple.

"You'll have to pay for that glass!" threatened my father, punctuating his words with an index finger. I thought to myself: *he must be kidding!* I was only eleven years old with no income of any kind, let alone pocket money.

Where does he think I'm supposed to get the money from? It's almost like he was in my head because I remember him saying, right after that thought: "tomorrow you are coming with me to work." The following day he woke me up early and off to work we went.

Not knowing that tomorrow, just one day, would turn into more than 2190 days working to pay for that glass. Keep in mind this was an ordinary white refrigerator, not a golden throne.

How was I to work out how a glass shelf broken by a pre-teen in her own home was to equate to six years of slavery? In no time this 11-year-old little girl, powerless in the face of her taskmaster, was carting wheelbarrows full of raw bricks from one production station to the next. If I filled my wheelbarrow halfway instead of to the top I could expect a good slap for my trouble. If he failed to land the slap to his liking he would stand me up straight and tell me to hold still. The second delivery would be more to his liking, spinning the head off my shoulders. And as if that was not good enough he would proceed to his favourite part of the exercise—the manhandling.

He would collar me by the neck and savagely yank me this way and that like a rag doll till I lost my footing and landed face down in the clay. At first I had no idea where I got the strength to wheel that wheelbarrow. What I can tell you is the definition of full. The brim was not it! I had to lift a load his workers were not able to lift, and not for lack of trying.

Ask any builder or contractor about raw bricks, because of the water content their density is far greater, therefore way heavier. There I was crying uncontrollably, hoping my father would have mercy on his daughter, since my debt clearly wasn't paid by now. The more I cried, the angrier he became. Now I was making noise and drawing unnecessary attention to us, yes, us! Days became weeks and weeks became months and I grew accustomed to it.

I stopped crying and got used to carrying the mountainous load— this was me accepting my new normal. From here I developed what we can call built-in power, or shall I call it intrinsic power? Either way, I strongly believe that we are all born with power buried down in the inside of each of us—and you are no exception.

I had an insane theory that kept me going all those years—you can bend anything to your own will, only if you are hungry enough. In my case, I was hungry enough to avoid the slapping, the manhandling and the threats about more beatings.

I had to tap into a realm I was aware of but couldn't comprehend at the time. It is in that realm, that mental state, that I got to discover the magnitude of the power that lay within me.

Don't ask me how I knew that from a young age, but I did. It's what I mean by one-of-a-kind. To put my insane theory to the test I found an intriguing analogy, a certain Professor Alexander Eigeles Emanuel, a leading electrical engineer in the US. He says "the intrinsic power is an instantaneous non-active power always present when the active power is present." He sums it up in electrical language:

> "The intrinsic power is an instantaneous power with the following characteristics:
> 1. Always present when active power is present, except for direct current systems with zero voltage and current ripple.
> 2. Under steady-state conditions, the intrinsic power does not cause net transfer of energy to the load, nor is causing power loss in active materials, over N-cycles duration.
> 3. Does not affect the apparent power value."

His closing words: "When powers are studied it is necessary to recognize the intrinsic power as an inconsequential power and not to confuse it with other types of active powers." Bearing in mind that he was talking about the power of electricity, not human beings, I am taken aback to discover a connection between the human construct and energy. It is bewildering to consider that our intrinsic power performs exactly like energy! In just the same way intrinsic power exists for energy when a demand is made on it, our intrinsic power is and has always been ready for when we make a demand on it. Before you consider giving up or giving in to your depressing circumstances before you consider suicide as I did, or a pity party, first make a demand on your intrinsic power—it is readily available for you. Just because you don't feel it doesn't mean it does not exist! Like energy, there is no evidence of such a thing under normal conditions.

But just because it is non-active doesn't mean it is non-existent. It is unlimited, has neither height nor depth, leading me to be convinced that the same power that raised Jesus from the dead and released him from a sealed tomb lives inside of us! And that must be the source of our intrinsic power. If the tomb could not contain Him, if death could not hold Him back, what is holding you back?

Again you may consider the principle of faith and what faith it is that moves mountains. What energy is released by throwing our full power into whatever insurmountable obstacles standing before us? What power is unleashed when we do so, depending not on our own strength but relying rather on a power outside of ourselves, but released in us, through us? Looking back at how my adversity began and how the torture was perpetuated over time instead of lessening off, I came to a fair conclusion about life—that the challenges we face don't get easier, we only become stronger.

What no one tells us is, being stronger comes at a price, it sets us up for more challenges as we reach new heights in our lives. Strength is a double-edged sword; with great strength comes an even greater responsibility. The world we live in demands us to be ever-stronger, both emotionally and physically. It's essential for success and survival. But as you build this unbreakable mental and physical fortitude, you also stand alone atop a mountain, gazing down at the people who couldn't quite make it, those who fell along the way. Being strong isn't just about muscles or intellectual capabilities. It's the resilience to face adversities, to take on life's most grueling tasks without crumbling under their weight. I am almost convinced that Samson (whom we commonly know as Delilah's boyfriend from the Holy Book) in Judges 16:30 knew about this fact, which is maybe why he was able to kill so many Philistines in his later days.

> *Samson said, "Let me die with the Philistines!" Then he pushed with all his might, and down came the temple on the rulers and all the people in it. So he killed more people when he died than he had during his entire lifetime.*

I wonder how many of us, understand that when our physical strength is gone, when we have our backs against the wall, that is when our intrinsic power work best. I can't help but suspect that when God was creating Adam in the beginning in Genesis 2: 7, he was depositing this power, which makes me strongly believe that it must be freely and readily accessible to everyone.

Then the LORD God formed a man from the dust of the ground and breathed into his nostrils the breath of life, and the man became a living being.

When others see your strength and wisdom, they will undoubtedly turn to you for help—which is both a gift and a burden. As you embrace the burden of strength, prepare yourself for the reality that life will only become more challenging. The bar is raised, and expectations are higher than ever before. People will look to you for guidance in times of trouble, seeking your unyielding spirit as they navigate through darkness. But remember this: with every challenge you conquer, with each difficulty you face head-on and overcome—a new level of resilience is unlocked within you. It shapes you into a formidable force that remains rooted against all odds. Embrace the price of being strong as an opportunity to experience growth beyond what many will know in their lifetime. As you break through limitless boundaries, remember that those challenges stand before us not to break us but simply test our resolve and reveal our true potential. So go forth and take on these hurdles with grace and determination. Learn from each obstacle and strive to become better—because when we are strong, we have a unique ability to help others find their strength too. Thank you for allowing me to share my thoughts on the price of strength and its ensuing challenges. As we journey together through life's gauntlet of trials, let us remember to stand tall and remain unbreakable. I wish I had known this when I became comfortable with that mountainous wheelbarrow and started moving it without concern for the load. Little did I know that the worst was yet to come, that an apple and a broken glass shelf was just the beginning of my nightmare.

2

Hellish prison

J ust when I was getting used to coping with my unbearable circumstances, my master gave me more responsibilities. When in hell, as they say, keep going. To tell you more about this I must tell you more about brick manufacturing. After drying, the bricks are fired to high temperatures in furnaces. During the burning process, the dried bricks are burned in brick clamps to a certain degree—between 1000° C and 1100 °C—for hardness and strength. To put it in context, only certain metals and alloys like stainless steel, nickel and titanium can withstand such heat. The cooling stage is the final phase in the brick manufacturing process. From there the bricks are moved to the display area and sold. In an ideal world, it takes several days for the fired bricks to cool down. They cool slowly in the open air so the process can take its course. But I wasn't living in an ideal world, you know. I was not yet a human being.

With customers waiting in the wings with hard cash my father would instruct his employee slaves to unpack the burned bricks from the brick clamp without a thought for the cooling process. I recall how antsy my master became with customers on-site, the way their cash turned him on—turned him red like the bricks—his eyeballs flickering to the left to right like flames from the furnace. He was like a puppy wagging his whole body for a bone being dangled before his nose. How could I escape as a spectator? How could God be so kind?

I was still watching them unpacking the bricks with heavy-duty gloves when I heard the voice.

"What are you waiting for?"

I stood there in disbelief... *does he expect me to touch those bricks?* and answering—*he must be mad.* There was just no way!

I was hoping he would listen to what he had just said and hear how insane it was to be saying it. I pretended not to hear, in the hope, he would. Next thing a hand on my neck like an iron collar, my slavemaster dragging me by the neck—"you're such a spoiled brat!"—and throwing me on the heated pile of bricks that still had traces of flames and burning ashes.

What hell was this now? And what was this thing of a spoiled brat? When or how was I ever a spoiled brat?

I have no idea what a spoiled brat is unless it is a human being that escapes the suffering of hell and the abuse I suffered as a child. If that is a spoiled brat I am a spoiled brat and think every one of us should be. I knew what he meant by throwing me on the heap. I knew there was no point in denying him or defying him. But I never knew what he meant when I asked him for the heavy-duty gloves his employees used.

"You're such a spoiled brat," he said again. "I will teach you a lesson." Whatever the lesson was and whatever I had done wrong was immaterial. The bricks were literally on fire still from the furnace and I was to load them with my tiny bare hands. What was it about me? What was it about him? When even to say anything or to feel anything was a punishable offence. To not be able to express my feelings at all but to suppress them and become that feeling-less thing he was... it's like I was being punished for being born. Punished for existing. And to stop being a spoiled brat I had to stop existing. So the next stage in my development started. There was no going back to reason and rationalization. At that moment there was no bluffing. No bluffing him nor bluffing myself. Unbelievably, incomprehensibly, in denial of all that is human, I joined the crew with nothing but my bare hands. There's not much more I can say about it. Words don't seem to mean anything next to it.

My first attempt at packing the wheelbarrow was beyond my power like before. It took a few more slaps and punches and manhandling to reactivate my intrinsic power. The second was easier and the third and all the other loads that followed.

You'll understand—I confess—I used to think the Bible was a scam and had begun hating God for letting me go through such excruciating pain at the hands of my devilish parents. But I came across this text in Exodus 1:8-11 doing Sunday School homework:

"Then a new king, to whom Joseph meant nothing, came to power in Egypt. "Look," he said to his people, "the Israelites have become far too numerous for us. Come, we must deal shrewdly with them or they will become even more numerous and, if war breaks out, will join our enemies, fight against us and leave the country. So they put slave masters over them to oppress them with forced labour, and they built Pithom and Rameses as store cities for Pharaoh. But the more they were oppressed, the more they multiplied and spread; so the Egyptians came to dread the Israelites and worked them ruthlessly. They made their lives bitter with harsh labour in brick and mortar and with all kinds of work in the fields; in all their harsh labour the Egyptians worked them ruthlessly."

Strange how a Bible text from nowhere that told a story about a suffering people from so long ago reached me as if it were happening then—and indeed it was—to me. The thought sent a shiver down my spine. From that moment it dawned on me that my father was doing all these things because he was trying to kill the person he knew I could be—the person he knew he could never be. He wanted to break me down so he could create a version of me that wouldn't be a threat to him. What he underestimated though was the power of the soul.

There is something magical about the soul that can carry a wounded body when it can no longer carry on.

When your mind starts to believe that maybe you are a slave and then your soul steps in and silences every voice that is not true about who you are. It's like my soul knew who I was way before I could connect the dots for myself— before I knew who I was. And just like the Israelites, the more he came at me, the stronger I became. The stronger I became, the more frustrated he got. When calamity strikes, regardless of what direction it's coming from, it's not there to kill you but to strengthen you. God is a God of multiplication, not subtraction. It's not a function of *if* but *when.* So when you reach the end of your season of calamity—the end of one crisis after another after another— you come out multiplied. Not only multiplied in strength but wisdom, resilience, humility, and most of all, faith. I often tell my clients that in the face of adversity, calamity, and struggle, we can find strength and purpose. That each moment of difficulty is not designed to break us but rather to remind us of our inherent ability to rise above. Calamity has been a constant companion throughout human history. It knocks on our doors, unbidden and often unwelcome, bringing with it heartache and suffering. But what if I were to tell you that these challenges we face are not meant to kill us but instead to strengthen us? Just as iron is forged by fire and pressure, so too are we shaped by the experiences that test us. Each trial makes us stronger, more resilient, more able to withstand the trials that lie ahead.

We are like oak trees with deep roots that sway but never break against raging storms. The key lies in how we view these adversities when they come our way. Do we perceive them as unfair burdens designed to bring us down? Or do we see them as opportunities for growth, for learning about ourselves and our capabilities? When we choose the latter perspective, something truly transformative happens within us. We feel a renewed sense of purpose and direction—a passion for life that envelops our very being. Suddenly, we are no longer victims of fate but rather masters of our destiny. Let me share with you an important truth: every calamity in your life is there for a reason. It whispers in your ear and teaches you something about your hidden strength you may not have previously known. Embrace its lessons with open arms; learn from them; emerge stronger and wiser than before. Remember that every storm eventually passes. The rain subsides, the clouds part, and sunlight soon filters through once more. Calamity is not your enemy; it is the crucible in which your true potential is revealed. Cherish the journey, even when it brings with it challenges and obstacles, for in the end, it is these experiences that will shape the person you become. That is what I would say to the 11-year old girl, in retrospect. *Life is beautiful. There are lessons to be learned in every pain. Wisdom, resilience, humility and faith look good on you little warrior.* Those are the words I use to comfort the wounded child in me. I carry her with me wherever I go, with honour and sensitivity. She is my role model—I look up to her more than I do to anyone else. She is teaching a 33-year-old me so much about life, I love her. She is fragile yet so strong. Without discounting and invalidating her pain and trauma or giving credit to her abusive parents, it was good for her to be afflicted that she may know how strong and resilient she is.

What I also learned about adversity and crisis is, it doesn't make us, it reveals who we've been this whole time, just without knowing it. But how many of us know these things at the time? And how many of us know what we could do about it if we knew better? I recall the first time I showed my burned hands to Elizabeth. They were full of wounds, blisters and blood but somehow they were not enough to move her. What kind of a mother you may ask, what social worker? "You will have to go back to work," she said after dressing me up with bandages and ointments from work. Deep down I was not surprised by her lack of compassion and empathy. Then I tried with old rags but there was no escaping the heat, they would catch fire immediately, exposing my hands again. Another thing you must know, my slavemaster was the laziest person you could ever meet. Or he suffered a work allergy-like nothing the doctors had seen before. You'd swear he was physically incapable, that he had a few arms or legs missing, or had suffered a stroke, or been involved in an accident that left him paralyzed from the waist down. He would have been better off with a wheelchair, any kind of chair, anything to facilitate sitting in the sun all day and doing nothing. Between the love of doing nothing and the love of money, he lived in-between, in no man's land. Here again, we can talk about masters. You can't serve two masters. You can't serve God and Mammon. The problem was Mammon. He worshipped at the feet of Mammon. While calling himself a follower of Jesus. There's hypocrisy and there's blasphemy, if that is not blasphemy then you tell me what is. Taking the name of Christ and doing exactly the opposite of what Christ would do. Taking His name and dragging it through the mud. He loved his money god so much he would have killed for it. It would have killed him also if he didn't have it. So between the two he would never come on-site to see who was stealing from him or lazing around but hang around nearby and watch from a distance: close enough to keep an eye on the production line but far enough not to get his hands dirty. There was this couple working with me that had worked for him for as long as I can remember—roughly 20 years. They would use the unsupervised window periods to lend me their heavy-duty leather gloves to provide me with some form of relief. But here's the fact about temporary relief, unless you get rid of the core of the problem, your reality remains unchanged. Getting the relief from them now and again didn't take away my pain. Quite frankly, it made no difference. I knew I had to find a way out of this hell.

When in hell, keep going. I tossed up my different options. Relatives were not on the list. Aunts, uncles, grandparents, it was a foreign world to me. Family and love were not in my world, in theory or in practice. To this day, one of the best ways I spend my time is in my head. It all started in hell, in my clay pit prison, at such a tender age. Since the church was no help, nor Social Services, the police were no help either. The odds were against me. No one would believe a determined (obnoxious) wilful (cheeky) no push-over (rude) child over two saints that went out of their way to help the church congregants when they had problems with their children at home. They were very convincing, would always be. The first to get to church and the last to leave—the perfect couple. You could say they were "serving faithfully in the house of the Lord." They didn't stop at serving but were the first always to pay money they never had for whatever church reason. If it was me watching from some other place far away from me I would have wondered why the lavish outlay. What lay behind all this furious generosity? If not a desire to impress, or suppress? To impress others and distract them from the truth and suppress what was happening at home and inside themselves? My hatred for marriage and what it represented continued to grow as I watched the ongoing hypocrisy. I swore to myself that I would rather die than get married and have children. Parenthood was no different to murder so far as I could see. I knew I was not capable of such cruelty, therefore it was best not to have children—not if having children meant becoming so cruel and wicked to them, showing no mercy, and sowing the same seeds of cruelty and wickedness in them. Where was I to run? Where was I to go? Where was the place I could escape to, apart from the place in me, the place inside my head?

At this stage I stopped trusting, I stopped trusting people and I stopped trusting dogs. I had no living thing to look to as a friend, it was me and my shadow. The dogs seemed to know it as well, or as well as, any of my neighbours. Any man on the street could not have known more, or cared less, than any dog. On this particular day I decided to get out, to make my break, to live on the streets but I found myself back in prison quickly. God knows what was up with the dogs that day, and the human beings. Like they knew I did not belong there. Suddenly, it was like a rival leader out of nowhere signalled his gang and they all came charging in a pack. A pack of dogs were all over me, they started licking me like I was some dead meat. I tried different streets that day but got the same outcome each time. I'm still living with a dog phobia, I can't forget that day with me in the dust and dirt of the road with them all over me, nipping at me and yelping and biting and growling and snapping and plucking at me curled up in a ball with my head in my chest and screaming to I don't know who, because there was nobody. "It takes a community to raise a child" they say, where was the community that day when I feared for my life? When all I had to fight my fear was my fear? To them it was just another street show. It was not funny back then, but I love joking about how I almost became a street kid but my operation failed because I didn't have the technical know-how. My failed attempt to break out was quickly endorsed by my reality. To pivot perhaps was the answer here, to direct my energy into books instead of trying to escape. If I could secure good grades I could secure a bursary, then what? Nothing was impossible to me, all I had to do was imagine it. It worked out that way, just as I imagined. I performed exactly as planned, fuelled by my thwarted plans to escape. I threw myself into my books and who knows if that was not where the dogs had been chasing me? On top of my class, on top of my school, year in, year out, despite the fact that I was denied my studies at home. And to reward me for escaping the dogs my slavemaster threw me to the pigs. He was also into piggery. To this day my memory has gaps when it comes to this chapter of my life—there is no amount of counselling or hypnotists that can erase the horrendous trauma of having pigs licking your face and your body, everyday like you're some piece of a dead dog. I can't tell you how I got recruited there, no one else will either. Elizabeth refuses to talk about it. Her husband claims he can't remember. What I can tell you: I was still figuring out my move after failing with the dogs when he threw the pigs at me. Two decades later, I still get nightmares about it. They say time heals everything—I say bull crap. Time does not heal everything. Time makes you see things differently. Time makes you feel better. Time helps you move on. You may look like you have healed for some time, until one trigger, then it sets you back to the trauma. My triggers are pets. The minute their fur touches my skin I lose my mind, I go cray cray it actually gets embarrassing. My mind, as I say, was my safe place, my only place, but now the pigs were there and the pigs were hungry. The pigs were in my place and my place was the place of the pigs. Did he not intend it that way, the pig who put me there? I mean, is there no Bible story I am not in? This one is The Prodigal Son. The pigs became not only my trigger but my trauma. They would step on me and bowl me over and sit on me and cover me with mud as I tried feeding them. I started having nightmares so bad every night that I dreaded going to bed. Between the nightmare of night and the nightmare of day I could not tell between pig and nightmare. My night and day were all one as my pig and pig were all one.

But still, you adjust and you cope and you step up and you manage. You rise above your hell and keep going. After all, 12 is not that young not to be a warrior. He noticed, and added more responsibilities. The last straw proverb he took literally, but for a mule. 50 kg of pig food—I was just over half that weight myself—and if I murmured or looked for help from anyone… the rod. It all sounds impossible now, how can a 12-year-old lift a 50 kg bag of pig food? How can a child, a girl child, carry the weight of a man? What man himself, a working man, could carry it? Then again, more responsibilities. I must mix the food to specifications, to the preference of his pigs, when I got home. So much of this and so much of that and exactly this and exactly that, or else. I was no longer his daughter I told myself. He was no longer my father. He was my master and I was… still figuring it out. How much more? *No end to how much more. No end to how low we can go.* I was in a hurry one day and didn't mix the pig food according to specification and my master discovered it.

"Would YOU eat it?"

No response.

From there on I remember only blackness, blindness, fighting for air, for my life, my face shoved into the pig food.

"EAT IT! EAT IT, YOU LITTLE BRAT! EAT IT!"

Around this time I held an emergency meeting in my head. Me, myself I. Against the world. Something had to be done. I meditated long and hard, call it premeditation. I was going to get rid of him permanently, I said. *Burn him alive. End the nightmares. Put a stop to all this madness. There's nowhere else to go.* I had his murder orchestrated at the age of 12 and a wonderful story rehearsed for the cops, my mother, and the church congregants. None of our neighbours cared about him. I'm sure they saw through him. They were no saints either. My neighbourhood was more like a hub of shenanigans, they just varied in degrees. Setting a trap for my master had to be one of the easiest things to do—he was tediously brainless and predictable. No one should underestimate a 12-year-old! Or a three year old for that matter—considering how dangerous a three year old can be, remembering everything. Hearing him cry like a helpless baby that day, as I set him on fire showed me how much of a coward he was. I wish no hell on anyone but no one must wish me in hell. To my surprise he came out with second-degree burns on his thighs and legs. I had planned for nothing less than his immolation. Death by fire was the best I could come up with at the time. I only know I wanted him to die a slow, painful death while I watched, enjoying the reversal of roles. Ask any victim of prolonged violent abuse, you sit and day dream about different ways of killing your abuser while making sure they suffer in the process. There are no accidents here, it's all premeditated. It's what WE call justice. Call it what you will, I'm not promoting violence, I'm merely giving you a sneak peak of what goes on in our heads when enough is enough. When violence has been perpetuated on you your whole life and now it comes your turn to see justice. This must have been my happiest memory as a child. Judge, don't judge, it's inconsequential to the 12-year-old me. The funny thing is, you would have never seen a slave back then. I never took myself for a slave, only a little girl with a master. For me, the mindset was everything. At times, we may feel like our circumstances define us, that we are merely products of the environment we're born into. However, allow me to remind you today that this is not true. Our circumstances do not determine who we are or who we are destined to become. Each one of us has the power within ourselves to rise above our challenging situations and adversity. We possess the strength and determination to change the course of our lives by reshaping our thoughts, actions, and perspectives. As it says in Proverbs 23:7 - "As a man thinks in his heart, so is he." This verse teaches us that it is our thoughts, beliefs, and convictions that truly define us. Our resilience and faith will guide us through these challenging times. Let's continue to dream big, work hard, and never give up on ourselves. Let us keep in mind that it's not where we come from or what circumstances surround us that determines our destiny; it's who we become by overcoming those very circumstances. Our hearts and minds have limitless potential—hold onto hope and embrace your built-in power. As young as I was, I refused to be defined by my circumstances. There was no element of self-pity or need to be comforted—I knew who I was and where I was going, it was only a matter of when. I was, and still am, one-of-a-kind. You look at me now and you see a queen, a lioness, totally in control, in command of her kingdom. Seated in her domain, she looks out on the world.

3

Slip of the tongue

I t came as a surprise when my little sister and I were sent to Hofmeyer for the school holidays. Our father was from Hofmeyer, approximately 60 kilometres away. His mother and sister—Emily, Eunice—were so fond of the home town they never left. With Emily it allowed her to be close to her mother, Ouma. She was blessed to live a long life and was the only great-grandmother I ever knew.

Eunice and her husband were blessed with two children—their house was not far from where Emily lived. Ouma's house, on the other hand, was more of a refugee camp, I can't tell you how many grandchildren, great-grandchildren and cousins she sheltered under her roof. My sister and I—along with Emily—would make frequent visits to Ouma's house when we were in Hofmeyer. We'd go back to Emily's house for playtime with Ouma's great-grandchildren. Emily was looking after Eunice's two children, which meant every day she had to come by to pick them up. It was a much-needed break for me being away from a toxic environment—living in constant fear from when the next beating would be and from which angle.

The fact that I didn't have to look over my shoulder every minute of every day came with a huge sense of relief for me. I was also able to explore and play with other children on the street without coming back home to be welcomed by uncalled-for assaults and being reminded that I had broken some imaginary rule by playing on the street. At home, my sister and I were caged for as long as I can remember. The rules were very clear: we play with our neighbours' children through the fence. To attempt any more than that was another reason to chase our friends away. This didn't stop us from having a taste of normal childhood when we could—we capitalized on our parents being away at times during the day and joined in for street games when we could. Our friends were all aware of our predicament and the repercussions thereof—we'd all be on the lookout for our parents as we were playing, planning our exit strategy depending on the game. Here's the thing, because we were living on a mountain we had a bird's view of the comings and goings of pretty much everyone and everything in our small township. The reverse was also true—it meant they could also see what we were up to if they bothered to look up. "Wise as a serpent," it says, "innocent as a dove". If it was street soccer on the day it would mean kicking the ball intentionally toward our house while my little sister took cover behind one of the bigger players. I'd pull the goalie's long and oversize coat over me while making a run for the ball. We'd all gather at the gate to obstruct the view while my sister and I slipped through and around the back to get in through the windows while the goalie took the match back to the street in his coat.

We were living like caged animals, with no access to social life. Hofmeyer, in comparison, was like paradise. Taking long walks on the streets, going nowhere, was a dream come true. Except the dream was quickly shattered for me. It must have been the excitement of hosting that caused Emily to cook and dish up for us every day, with no agenda. It started one night with *pap en vleis* (putu pap and meat)—our local favourite. As the plates came out of the kitchen one by one I received the shock of my life. I looked down on my plate with a pile of bones on a mountain of pap with a few drops of gravy. I couldn't help but look around me. My little sister had a lion's share, so did my cousins. I wasn't sure whether to be bothered or take it as an oversight. You want to believe the best, hope for the best when you are with your family. You want to feel like you are part of that family. But the following day my suspicions were confirmed. There could be no doubt. Again I received a few drops of soup on my mountainous pap while everyone's soup covered their pap nicely.

My alarm bells started going off right there and then, this felt familiar—and just when I thought my father's family was different! It was as if a memorandum had been issued that week! It was on a Friday when my aunt Eunice came for after-work drinks to Emily's house. She brought in a grocery bag full of goodies—and a street load of attention and anticipation.

I'm not sure how cruel people need to be to show us they are cruel. I don't know what cruelty was done to them for them to want to be cruel in turn.

I'm not sure if I can ever be so cruel, if I can, God help me. She took out chips, chocolates and biscuits and distributed them to all the children in the house—starting with hers and my other cousins—while ignoring me. "Give that bastard child whatever you feel like, if you feel something at all," she said as she threw herself on the sofa. "I don't even know why she's here, to begin with," she said softly, taking a sip of beer. Her slip of the tongue opened my mind to a whole new world. A world built on lies. I was smart enough for my age, worldly-wise, but not once did it occur to me this was not my father. I guess I had no reason to suspect I was a bastard child because my biological mother was just as cruel to me, only passively. I had no reason to suspect that I was unwanted until Emily and Eunice enlightened me. Suddenly it all made sense! No wonder Ouma was so cold to me from day one. I remember thinking she was old and that must have been the reason she didn't talk. But then she'd talk to her other great-grandchildren, Eunice's children, and I'd be confused.

She wanted me to know where she stood with me, or rather, where I stood with her. It was barbaric, yes, having no bearing on me. I'd rather be resented and be left out in the cold than to be resented and tormented. But Ouma was old school. I'm convinced her reaction to me had a lot to do with the generation she represented. She knew it was pure evil to let your inner struggles spill over onto an innocent child—even if you wanted nothing to do with that child. She kept her hands clean I can say, she had no blood on her hands, no innocent child to account for, may she rest in peace. But I had never felt so foolish.

It was official.

I didn't belong.

Period.

My parents got married in 1989, I was born in August that same year. Every time I asked Elizabeth about the details surrounding my birth I got different answers. But when I asked about my little sister and brother she would give me the same responses, even with her eyes closed.

I became like a dog with a bone, I kept seeking answers until she threatened me. "Stop starting what you cannot finish," she said. I discovered that a DNA test was required by my paternal family, what I didn't discover was the reason for denying them one. Elizabeth refused to do a paternity test which begs the question: why be afraid of the truth that is already out sin the open? The truth that was found in actions more than 30 years ago? What did she stand to gain for staying in such an abusive marriage?

Enduring not only domestic and mental abuse but financial abuse too? I wonder how many other women, are still living in condemnation because of sins they had committed long ago? Elizabeth must have had a different definition of grace. I don't think there's anyone that says it better than Paul who goes by the street name of Saul in Romans 8: 1-2,

"So now the case is closed. There remains no accusing voice of condemnation against those who are joined in life-union with Jesus, the Anointed One."

Her sin was forgiven, her case was closed but she still walked around with the weight of her past, causing her more harm than good. You may not be Elizabeth, but let me ask you, what mistakes are still chaining you to the past? Why are you paying an interest on a debt that was settled not even decades but centuries ago? "Have you not known? Have you not heard? The everlasting God, the Lord, the Creator of the ends of the earth, does not faint or grow weary; there is no searching of His understanding." Bring your shenanigans to Him.

He's Holy enough to handle your dirty secrets,

He's holy enough to handle your ugly truth,

He's holy enough to forgive your sins,

He's holy enough to pardon your in equities,

He's holy enough to sanctify you,

He's holy enough to love you unconditionally.

4

The sins of the mothers

Immediately the scales were off my eyes I started seeing things for what they were, not what I'd hoped for. Instead of secretly hoping for acceptance from Elizabeth, one day I had to face the ugly truth that my parents never wanted me. It was clear that my father was never my father and he hated me for it. The feeling was mutual—there was no love lost there. Seeing me every day must have been like a constant reminder of what Elizabeth seemed to be fighting so hard to forget—a memory she would rather die with than to tell—while to my monster of a step-father I was nothing but a betrayal on two legs. The betrayal that Elizabeth must have caused him somehow made him suffer so deeply that it spilt over to me. I realized that my suffering was only a reflection of a turmoil that was brewing within him.

A lot of things started to make sense, it now made sense why he used to call Elizabeth a whore for as long as I can remember, and ended up calling me a whore. He must have felt weak and unmanned for his girlfriend, soon-to-be wife, to be impregnated by another man. What was done to him by her he was now going to do to me, the copy of her. From as early as three my childhood was stolen from me to pay a debt I never incurred—a debt that had nothing to do with me—a debt these two wilfully transacted in.

What I can now call my step-father stepped up to play God in my life, punishing me for what he deemed as the sins of my mother. We all know about the sins of the fathers—"I am a jealous God, visiting the iniquity of the fathers upon the children unto the third and fourth generation" as it is written. We see here how important the role of a father is, how responsible he is, how he is held accountable. But no mention of the mothers and what the mother does to influence her child either way. I can never speak for my mother or draw conclusions based on unfounded assumptions but it seems like she made up her mind that my conception will be one thing that remains between her and God. She has refused and still will refuse to talk about it, only reply with a church hymn—name your favourite. I had always been good at minding my own business but when it came to her I felt entitled: like she owed it to me for every stripe on my back and every slap and kick to tell me the truth. I had been more than a sacrificial lamb in her definition of marriage. I'd been a scapegoat for adultery and the victim of extreme abuse—in the home of a social worker!

I remember this one afternoon, borderline evening, a tall dark guy came to our house while my sister and I were busy playing outside. He greeted us and asked if Elizabeth was home. We answered him "yes" and he walked to the front door and knocked, then let himself in. It was the most logical thing to do with the door open and the person you were coming to see sitting in the dark right across from you. It was not a social visit because he didn't spend more than two minutes at the most before he left. When my step-father arrived back from his church meeting and received our usual report back of the day he called me into the kitchen to show him the exact spot where the man was standing when he spoke to Elizabeth.

He started drawing lines on the floor and asking me a multiple-choice question I couldn't possibly answer since I wasn't there and didn't see. "Where was he standing, here, here or here?"

I knew then, as you know by now, that whatever I said would still get me punished—punished for another sin I didn't commit. The insanity of it. Nothing to do with me. But an excuse must be invented to take out his devils on me.

Bang!

He shoved me up against the wall, hammering my head against the brickwork. Then the kitchen table he took for a battering ram and pinned me against the wall. I must tell him where the mystery man was standing, he said, while he hammered the table into my abdomen. *Bang! Bang!* Back and forth, back and forth, ramming it into my body like a corrupt cop forcing a confession out of an innocent bystander. The interrogation continued to the tune of table legs scraping along the floor and screaming in my ears and an index finger jabbed into my nose. He was somehow convinced that me pinned up against the wall would get an answer out of me.

"How many times must I tell you never to leave your mother with a man in my house when I'm not here?" he raged. As if I'd seriously heard that instruction before.

It was like when I was falsely accused when he made up excuses to get all psycho on me. I was his prey every time he got bloodthirsty. I was hardened by this time to assaults but I felt something move inside me next time the table came ramming into my abdomen. *Bang!* No matter what power I summoned he was going to bludgeon me here in the kitchen to a bloody pulp. I wonder here about sacrifice and how much I saved my little sister—how much she benefited from my suffering. She was old enough to be interrogated like I was but she was left in peace as usual. Just the fact we were playing outside would have told you he was not home—he didn't like us playing in the yard either. It was later I discovered it was me playing he had the problem with, not her. I found out she would play in the street whenever I was not home—a secret she didn't mind keeping. Again, the cruelty of human beings on human beings, innocent of wrongdoing. The sense of injustice that any one of us would feel who were only ever looking for love and protection from our parents. She got the best pairs of school shoes and best of everything while I was always told there was no money when I asked for things for school, mere basics. My little sister always had a backpack for school, while I had to carry my school books in a plastic bag. Plastic bags back then were not easily accessible, so if it was worn out it meant carrying my books using a DIY plastic bag made up of different pieces of plastic bags. I repeated this cycle until my plastic bags were beyond recyclable. Then again, there are levels of favouritism. I experienced a level that was well-calculated and direct at home but tactically inconspicuous to the person looking on from the outside.

My parents would have excelled in the Public Relations industry if they had known about it—it came naturally to them. They had PR smiles for church applied at the gate and default smiles they switched back to as soon as they left the church premises. When he accidentally bumped into my friends and me after school he would shower us all with R100 notes. That was a lot back then for little girls—way too much still in this day and age. My friends would tell me how lucky I was to have such a loving father that can just shower me with so much money without having to earn it. Such idiotic remarks were water on a duck's back to me. What they didn't know was every December when we went family shopping my parents would buy everyone new clothes—including themselves and my little brother— but not me. Come my turn it was them choosing for me and me paying for my clothes because I was working—I had a job remember? That was his way of taking back every last cent of the wages he had paid me in front of his workers—people from our church who could have reported him. Like any crooked cop, he had carefully calculated every move and created alibis where he needed them—it was always going to be his word against mine. You know by now whose side Elizabeth would choose. The only clothes they would buy me were church clothes, as they shopped for my siblings—the best and most stylish clothes ever. The price tags were exorbitant too, so money wasn't the problem. Thinking about it you wonder if subconsciously they were not trying to paint a picture of equity, trying to cover up for the injustice and favouritism at home. Outside of church, I had to pretty much fend for myself, I was a girl who was known for oversize, hideous hammy-downs (hand-me-downs)—from second-hand school shoes from my friends to second-hand shorts for athletics. I was no good at sports but with athletics, I felt comfortable. But my parents being my parents couldn't be bothered to buy me at least the cheapest running shoes—I had to run barefoot on a gravel sports ground throughout the five years that I participated in athletics. Some of my friends would take off their running shoes as they assumed running barefoot was somehow what made me win. When we competed against private schools Elizabeth would be the first to remind me to borrow a pair of running shoes from my friends. That showed me that she was aware of my running and certainly knew that you run using running shoes. But she was more concerned with how it would look—that her daughter doing so well would make her mother look bad. Running without shoes at an event like that would embarrass her. My sister on the other hand would name it and she'd have it. On competition days I would be selected to represent my school. I'd ask for pocket money on the day and they would refuse. Not surprised, I'd make home-made bread and cook chicken on the stove and trade them for treats with my friends. I probably did that twice or three times before I was told I wasn't allowed to touch "his" chicken any more. It was the same with the drink-o-pop that I would make and leave to freeze overnight—no space in the freezer he said, I must stop what I was doing. I could sense his exasperation from a distance—the more I wasn't bothered by his pettiness the more incensed he became. He would go to great lengths to set me up for humiliation—only to be humiliated himself. It all got too much—not the pain per se but the toxicity of living under the same roof as him. I was getting tired of getting tired.

I wanted to die—just not in his filthy hands.

Nor in my mother's arms either.

II

Part Two

Through my childhood window

5

I hate peanut butter

One of the toughest questions I've always failed to answer to my therapist is: "What is your earliest happy memory as a child?" I could easily tell her all about my earliest horrendous memories—I didn't have one, I had a plethora. I often hear people talk about the exhilarating feelings of moving to a new home and how sentimental they would be about parting ways with their old homes which were not just homes but incubators of happy memories. I guess I am not like them because I remember my first time being introduced to peanut butter at home—one of the memories I wish I never had. I vaguely recall the curiosity I had when I saw this poop-like spread being licked by Elizabeth—my mother, from the bread knife. I couldn't wait for my taste buds to prove my assumptions wrong.

My taste buds, unfortunately, proved my assumptions right. I can't tell you how much I had as my first, hesitant, bite… but I remember sprinting to the back door to throw up. It was the most nauseating bread spread ever. On returning indoors my step-father scolded me and warned me to stop wasting food as "money did not grow on trees." He forced me to eat my sandwich and threatened to punish me if I didn't finish it. Strangely, I should remember so far back—marvellous perhaps. I was over the age of two but not turned three yet—not old enough for daycare. I gladly took my sandwich outside, went straight to the fence, and called for Pauline. Pauline must have been a year or two older than I was, with the most beautiful big brown eyes. She had a cousin, I remember, who was like an imaginary friend to us. I asked her to take the sandwich off my hands and discard it—that way I knew there wouldn't be any incriminating evidence. One could never be too careful when it came to my paranoid ex-cop step-father. He measured and marked all the food in and around the house every night before he went to bed and would discreetly do his audits before we got up and then go back to bed. The same applied every time he had to step outside the house. Only he never knew he was not the only one with an aptitude for psychotic mind games.

My initial solution with Pauline ended up being a permanent arrangement. I don't know at what stage she decided to eat the sandwiches, I was only happy to suddenly get her jam sandwiches in return. I loved Pauline, not for anything else but for relinquishing a sandwich that tasted like free-range honey for a poop-tasting one. She was so swept away with peanut butter that she would call me over the fence and demand it. In turn, I would go back inside and ask for it even if I wasn't hungry—just to keep her happy—and keep the jam sandwich coming. It wasn't long before our organized crime was busted, of course. It was starting to get suspicious to any dummy paying attention to the details. I was not outsmarted, I maintain, but betrayed—by Pauline's addiction.

My step-father did what he did best: setting traps. He followed me without my knowledge and caught us red-handed. I had the jam around my moustache area and both my hands were sticky from it while Pauline was busy savouring her peanut butter. That is my last memory of Pauline. He must have slapped the memory right out of me.

He hit me so hard my head spun right around and I went momentarily blank. I guess I can say it started then, at the age of two, going for three. I was given strict orders to never speak to Pauline again and forced to eat peanut butter while he continued to slap me. The more bites I took, the more puke I spewed. The puke unleashed more puke.

"I hate peanut butter!" I screamed at him.

"You're such a spoiled brat!" he screamed back.

So the sporadic beatings moved to sustained assaults that would see me tangled in his long brown leather belt, slipping and sliding on my vomit. He told me to eat my vomit because no one was going to clean up after me. Stubbornness has never failed me, nor courage to resist. Spinning like a street dog in my vomit in my own house was punishment enough. I refused him, and from here, from "spoiled brat", came "cheeky". Despite the memory and despite my step-father I just don't have it in me to force my children to eat what they dislike, regardless of their reasons. I do, I confess, offer bribes for eating steamed broccoli and asparagus. Today they snack on lettuce and cucumber as easily as they would enjoy ice cream. But for me at their age peanut butter was just another reason to validate violently beating up on a toddler who was soon to become a preschooler.

My preschool days were another nightmare. Each day when I came back from school he would ask to see my books. For every letter I had erased at school—and got beatings for—I would get double beatings from him. It all depended on his mood. It was either slaps or his precious brown leather belt. Sloppy writing for a preschooler was a valid reason for corporal punishment to him. I wanted to vanish. I could just tell from a young age he detested me beyond words. He didn't even need to go out of his way to find something to punish me for. He would hit me and roll me on the ground all because I got home with the belt button of my school tunic on the right when he had put it on the left when I left for school in the morning. His hostility towards me had an element of obsession—my hair is a good example. I mean, I had a different nose, my face was another, but he could not leave my hair alone. I had attitude, sure enough, a sense of individuality—of self-respect and self-love that no level of abuse could deny—but really, it was my hair that triggered him. You may think he was obsessed or possessed or abstracted but here's the thing, not because he loved it or desired it but because it was personal to me—and what was personal to me must always be used against me. So what is considered beauty for a girl, and her asset, must be made to serve the opposite of that? And whatever beauty my face may have presented to the world, my hair must shut me up and hide me away. Then I think of the child in his hands, his hands like hammers and clubs, wielding whatever weapon it was. The child now the object of his hairdressing attention, the hands now wielding a comb. He would divide my hair at the crown and bring the front half down, savagely, hatefully, over my face. I was not to see and not be seen. In his mind, I would have not existed if there was no evidence I did. Where was Elizabeth, you may want to know? Well, she was not allowed to touch me unless it was for bandages and dressings—something she was professionally trained for.

How long? How long was I to be subjected to this ritual? I'm not sure what thing there is more personal to a girl than her hair—or her head for that matter. Each hair curling out from her scalp. Every hair that is numbered. And here he is with his sausage fingers plucking me around like a rag doll. So he would send me off to school covered up in front, covering not only my five-head (extra forehead) but my entire face. His obsession made no sense to me. And to remove the hair from my face, or to come home with anything different to what he had styled in the morning, well…he took that as invitation for corporal punishment.

I was only five years old when I started Sub A—Grade 1 nowadays—mature enough to understand my big old bully of a step-father, and survive him, but not old enough to keep up. I was chased away by my Bridge (now called Grade R) teacher, I was told, because I talked too much and had more questions than she had answers for. Then I was dumped within two weeks on my Sub A teacher. You could take this as a compliment but as I got older it made me realize that where I came from, speaking up was impermissible and punishable. And between the two—bridging home and school—was the rod.

I have no idea what it was with my step-father. I have watched whatever educational material there is on the subject. I have yet to see the hatred I saw in his eyes. Every time he would embark on the exercise of "punishing" me he would roll up his shirt sleeves and do a mini-meditation of sorts. I don't remember seeing him not sweating when he was working on me—he enjoyed every second of it. He would sweat so bad that he would call Elizabeth to bring a handkerchief—as if the sweat was somehow getting in his way, distracting him from his task. Under his arms it spread out to the front and back like some bottomless lake leaking out from his gut. I was not just his punching bag, I was his treadmill and gym-pal. It was like he found me to be the most convenient way to lose his despicable flab. He could barely breathe when he was done, which saved me—his heart couldn't handle it. But I knew he was not done yet when his lips were still trembling, his nose still puffed up and swollen and his eyes red and hungry for blood. My step-father was no human, that's all I know. Mama got married to a beast—a beast in appearance, a beast in brute strength, and a beast in cruelty and mentality. In short, the devil himself!

6

Rest in peace

The blunder of getting married to the devil himself comes at the expense of going from princess to prey. I can never know what attracted Elizabeth to that devil, a deep desperation for a sense of belonging comes to mind if I were to guess. She had a deep desire to be wanted, even if it came at the cost of losing herself in the process. Her biological mother, Smally, cared only for her first love, alcohol—and whatever man celebrated and facilitated her passion for it. This would explain her 8+ children, some with different fathers. I don't think she ever knew what day of the week it was, the passing of time was inconsequential to her unless it was with a bottle of some sort. Elizabeth's dad must have been familiar with his girlfriend's passions because he made sure before he died that little Elizabeth would be raised in a less reckless environment. Either she was special to her dad or her dad, like any good or decent dad, wanted to protect her from something. Perhaps it was the most diplomatic course to take, regardless. I say that because she told me she had a brother—uncle V and a sister—Lala from the same mother and father. Which begs the question: why her? Why not take all your three children if the environment was so destructive and their mother's credibility questionable? This was the double-question I asked many times, in different ways, hoping to get different responses, but failing each time. Her typical response to anything on this topic was to launch into a church hymn… *"Oh Lord my God…"* etc. During these times, I would witness her consciously switch from auto-pilot to mindfulness. Her responses were cloudy and vague and incongruous, fishing almost for a reply, but failing. Then the hymn. Like there was a trigger somehow, but I didn't know what it was. Her father's sister, Daphney, was barren. Daphney took her in and treated her like her own the best way she knew how. If this was voluntary or not remains a mystery. It's weird not to have my mother's childhood details, I know Daphney sent her to boarding school for a while and it was from my aunts later that I discovered she was passed on to her dad's uncle at some point.

The details surrounding the reasons and duration thereof were not forthcoming. When I would ask her about this part of her childhood it was back to *"glory, glory hallelujah."* When Daphney died I was there to see Elizabeth's reaction. Her colleagues were also there. They had to support her getting out of the car as she arrived home. She was ready to collapse and die herself. Evidently whatever feelings she had for her second mother were deep and real. She lost weight drastically in the days that followed—as if she was following Daphney to the grave. They moved her to the house where the body was so she would have time and space to receive visitors who had come to pay their respect. Also, it seemed like she wanted to grieve privately. Daphney was cold as a grandmother to us and a mother to Elizabeth. Who would blame Daphney for not knowing how to love someone else's child when she's never had her own? The interesting thing is, as I got older and wiser, I couldn't help but notice the motherly side of Daphney when interacting with my mother's cousins and their children—something that left me with questions I knew no one would have answers to.

What was it with Elizabeth that made her to be rejected to such great lengths by her family? I wonder how her life would have turned out if her biological dad hadn't died prematurely? How did it feel to be growing up in between worlds of neglect and rejection? Did she ever know the feeling of belonging? These are the questions I asked myself repeatedly as I started seeing the world differently. It didn't need a rocket scientist to figure out that the relationship she had with her second mother was one-sided. Either way, it's safe to say Elizabeth was happy to settle for anything that looked like love and warmth—it was clearly way better than Smally. There's a choice I see here that she had to make, between one and the other. And she chose the one that for her best represented what a mother should be. The fact that I had only formally met Smally three times growing up—only a five-minute walk away from us—says a lot. This was confirmed later when alcohol took its course and she was forced into sobriety. Elizabeth paid her only one or two visits a year—a Public Relations exercise. It was evident that there was no form of connection between the two of them. She was tiny, like Elizabeth (and like me), which explained her name. There were times when I would walk past Smally on the street without her recognizing who I was. I got tired of explaining myself whenever we met every second year. We were mere strangers joined by blood—nothing more. And when Smally died there was no mourning, only an offer to paint the house and revamp the dilapidated flooring—opposite to when Daphney died. Despite Smally's alcohol abuse she did manage to raise "normal" children. My older aunts may not have had the educational opportunities Elizabeth had but they are more mentally stable than her. They are not perfect, but they are perfectly normal—if there is such a thing—perfection is an illusion after all.

I couldn't help but wonder, could Elizabeth being the way she was have more to do with her second mother than her biological mother? Perhaps she grew up differently, protected from a reckless home, but what if that protection came at the cost of loneliness and rejection? Think about it. While her paternal family was everything her late dad thought she needed to be raised well, it seems to me that it did her more harm than good. It must be one of the most hurtful things to endure, to look to be accepted by people who had made up their minds about her long before she showed up. I can't imagine the heartbreak or imagine it being easy to forget, being tolerated instead of accepted, liked instead of loved. Yes, her paternal family may have liked her or accepted her as a child of their blood but they never embraced her as their own. They never loved her as blood, including her second mother. Was Elizabeth's new family guilty of being biased toward her and translating it into subtle prejudice? Did they resent her for sins she did not commit? Did she pose as a threat to their esteemed reputation? The questions keep coming. And we can only answer questions by asking questions. Or could it be that her innocence was somehow turned into filth, while her family turned a blind eye? I ask that because Daphney had a husband, which Elizabeth refused to talk about. The mention of his name would instantly result in a disgusted look on her face. I might not have the answers but I know that whatever the story is behind her trauma, must have been due to suffering at the hands of family. At times, it seemed to me like all she cared about was survival, whatever the cost she had to pay. I watched her trying so hard to gain their acceptance. It made me so mad, I can't explain it. They were her family but to them, she was never family. She was my mother but she was never a mother to me. Talk about the pain of pouring yourself out to death but still not being good enough in someone's eyes. The weird thing though, in the middle of this, I recall my Uncle V and Aunt Lala's short visits to our home. I'm not sure if they were there as customers or family since our house was a shebeen from dusk to dawn and home in between. Nevertheless, I was just happy to see them. Like my other aunts, they were both nothing like their sister. They were warm. They came over as often as they could and I would sit on my uncle's lap every time he came by—while my Aunt Lala would bribe me with tons of sweets—a treat I only experienced at home during Public Relations exercises. Lala looked more like Elizabeth's twin, except she was taller, like me. The three of them seemed very close, but it was short-lived. They both died prematurely, Lala from an HIV/AIDS-related illness. I was still a preschooler at the time. The only two people that ever treated me like family were taken away from me. I was ripped apart and knew it was over for me. I had no one to turn to. After all, no one expected a preschooler to grieve. I suppressed my grief for almost 30 years. Since so far back I've always had a thing against funerals and had no idea why. I must have been so traumatized by their passing that I don't even remember standing by their coffins to pay last respects to the two people God loaned me from time to time as a mother and father. My memory is blank so far as the timelines are concerned due to trauma. All I know is, after the one died I barely saw the other one again. My perfect idea of family was no more. Since then I have never attended funerals. I wonder if this is not the reason I became known as a deep child, insular, withdrawn. As a teen, I always found a way to dodge them—either by showing up late or availing myself for errands in the kitchen. It's like I was in denial of death, in denial of loss—the loss of love, the loss of hope.

"He has put eternity in our hearts," it says, not death. Death seems to go against our nature. But I have not changed, I still do not set foot at a funeral. It is only now as I write this that I discover why. There was no amount of therapy that could help me figure it out. May V and Lala's souls rest in peace.

The love they gave me during those short visits made my hell bearable. I was able to be a child in a child's body. They made me feel seen and heard. We were not just connected by Elizabeth's blood—it had to be something more than that. Growing up, I couldn't help but wonder if my situation would be different if they were alive. I knew I could trust them, I would have reached out to them for help. Instead, life went on at my home-cum-shebeen. I found myself watching intoxicated adults having explicit sex in front of a preschooler with no regard for the mental repercussions that took years to be pushed back—back to where I hoped they could be forgotten. One of the most disturbing yet normal scenes at home was watching different men sexually assaulting their girlfriends and wives. There was this pervert in particular who would stretch out his wife's legs on the floor outside our house and violently strip off her panties. He'd then take off his rugged twisted cap and throw it back before sticking his gigantic fingers inside her. I recall seeing him slowly licking the brownish fluids at the bottom of his index finger, working all the way up like he was indulging in a pudding. It must have been painful for the wife because she would beg him to stop while kicking and screaming. The louder she screamed, the more he seemed to be aroused. He would press her down as he would continue his revolting recreational activity. Until she'd give in and hold still, helplessly. At the time, I had no idea of what was going on. I don't think there's any preschooler that would. All I know is, it was agonizing. I remember the feeling of agony when my older step-brother came to visit us out of nowhere—my step-brother who spent most of his life either as a fugitive or behind bars. As I got wiser I realized that every time he came visiting he was hiding from the cops. You could say he had his PhD. in house burglary and armed robbery.

It must have been mid-week as Elizabeth and the beast were not home. It was around lunchtime when he closed all the curtains and doors. I was watching TV and couldn't be bothered. He picked me up and put me on my back on our green sofa, which was located right beneath the street-facing window, against the wall. He was already half-naked when he pulled up my dress and pulled down my panties. There was no suspecting anything since he always walked around the house and on the streets half-naked, showing off his tattoos. He told me to hold still while he quickly pulled down his pants and took off his red and white bucket hat with Scottish patterns. He had his knees either side of me when we heard Elizabeth's voice—only he didn't know her well enough to know her voice. He was still pushing to perform the deed when her hard knock at the door saved me. God showed up just in time—11:59:59—to save me from being raped by my step-brother. Elizabeth was a social worker specializing in cases of abused children, taking them away from their abusers, placing them in foster homes in an attempt to guarantee their safety.

Funny, right? She was not only passionate about saving abused children and fighting for them but she was also good at her job, trusted by her supervisors. It just so happened that on that day one of her clients was based in our neighbourhood. And since she was around, she stopped to have lunch.

Or?

God knows.

It was certainly no coincidence. It was a Godincidence. I've never believed in coincidences anyway. And maybe she did some good elsewhere that I do not know of, and God does. Perhaps some other child benefited. But you can imagine why she chose to be a social worker. It made me wonder how many of us run away from our realities, avoiding our inner demons, thinking the good we do to others will somehow serve to silence our demons?

7

Bloodthirsty

Apart from everything else I had to endure growing up I had to witness violence on a level I would not wish for anybody. "Peace on earth, goodwill toward men" was the plan. Not bloodshed and slaughter. "Thou shalt not kill," it says. But I wonder how much of that applies to life on earth. A life that has lifeblood. Certainly, there was no thought for that where I grew up. I remember things now I don't want to remember. I once witnessed a man being brutally stabbed to death with a piece of glass over his beer in our home-cum-shebeen while those sitting around watched for entertainment. Then the corpse just lied there in a pool of thick blood that soon set into a cherry-jelly substance before the cop showed up for *questioning*.

Here's the thing about where I come from: slaughter someone in the middle of the road in broad daylight, no one will *see* anything. But as a married man trying to sneak through your mistress' back window at 2 am, by 6 am the whole township knows. Elizabeth was heavily pregnant with her second child, my little sister, when her devil husband got bloodthirsty. She had made the mistake of confronting him about his precious mistress—only feeding the devil. He pulled no punches in reply, unleashing a fury of blows to her rib cage. "I dare

47

you to hit me" were her famous last words every time.

But this time the response was different. Lucifer was bloodthirsty. He threw her on the floor and kicked her, mopping the floor with her pregnant belly while she screamed for forgiveness. Then he picked her up and threw her out the window— the house was too small for his business. She landed on the sharp corners of the bricks outside, stacked diagonally for the flower garden she intended for our small backyard. The three-year-old-preschooler in me was convinced it was a heat of the moment thing, hot temper because I vividly recall him running, rushing towards the back door like he had come back to his senses and decided to miraculously catch her before she could land—if not for her sake, then for the baby. But he dragged her rather out the yard—mopping the gravel road with his heavily pregnant wife. I couldn't believe what I was seeing. Like I've said about my neighbourhood, a crowd came out to watch the scene—no one was willing to intervene, or save the helpless pregnant woman, or her innocent fetus. I remember a few elders begging him to stop— including Pauline's grandpa—but from a distance. Close enough to observe but far enough not to get involved. The beast would take small breaks between onslaughts to wipe off his sweat and roll back his sleeves.

He was not saying much all the while—only how disrespectful she was for confronting him. I was confused. Mama had to apologize to the cheater for cheating? Confronting your husband is disrespectful, yet cheating is not? What was I missing? Was he that sick, that demented and twisted? This was madness. Bloody madness. We couldn't tell where the blood was oozing from, only how excited and maddened he was by the sight of it—and no surprises to learn the spectators had called the ambulance, not the cops. Then a handful of men suddenly grew manhood in an attempt to stop what was going to be a straight murder. But he manhandled them like he was manhandling Elizabeth, unstoppable. I didn't want to witness another murder, no matter it was my mother. I walked away with others who found the scene unbearable. This is the point that cemented my hatred for marriage with every fibre of my being, swearing I would never have children. Between the traumas I was subjected to, being forced to absorb it all with my eyes, having to endure physical abuse, being unloved, uncared for, I don't know which one haunted me the most.

By the age of five I was already what society would label a solemnly damaged child. In my head, I thought there was nothing more that could possibly hurt me now, that there was no level of trauma beyond what I had endured already.

Elizabeth had been rushed to hospital. I don't have any details of what happened between the time I left and the arrival of the ambulance. If I were to guess, he must have stopped when his heart couldn't take it any more, as usual. Upon her return I was convinced she would kick him out—the house we were renting belonged to her cousin. I had started celebrating and imagining what my life would look like from thereon. I could smell my freedom, hear the sound of it if that's possible. It was a dream come true for me. I felt sorry for her on one hand but overjoyed also, coming out from under the power of a violent, vindictive and vile psychopath. But my bubble burst when she decided to make out as nothing had happened. The mistress was now a regular visitor to our house, any time of the day or night.

Elizabeth?

She did not object. One thing I never understood was seeing how the same man that was treating Elizabeth like trash would treat his mistress like a princess. "What does she have that I don't?" she would ask. I was equally curious. But no answer, only the usual slaps. I just can't say what she was thinking and feeling. Being taken for a laughing stock perhaps. But who was the laughing stock now? She cared too much about her image, always a prisoner of other people's opinions—what caused me to be the opposite from an early age. I was furious. I couldn't understand what could make someone so loyal. Was it even loyalty? Or was it simply a bleeding, bewildered young woman that didn't know any better? Either way, I felt betrayed by my own mother. Me being me I confronted her about it but she told me to stay out of her business. I told her it was my business too if it had a direct bearing on me. I was only three years old, but I was feisty as hell when I needed to be—come what may to try silence me. From the beginning, I had feared no man, used my voice like any man, and I feared no rod. "Cheeky" they called me, why? What did my cheeks have to do with it? Either way, it didn't change who I was becoming and who I cared not to become. She threatened to report me and my "absurd" suggestion to him. The absurdity was with her I told her. Was she bewitched? Elizabeth was financially independent, technically the breadwinner, while he spent all his money on mistresses. We had been renting my aunt's house and now I can well understand her decision to distance herself from her cousin and her toxic situation. She kicked us out. He moved next door into a property up for lease (he couldn't risk a relocation and subsequent loss of customers.) It was a commercial property with no privacy so we couldn't move in with him. Then my little sister was born, and to my surprise, as healthy as can be. No abnormalities! But it looked like Elizabeth was on her own, she was to fend for herself and her two children. It was commendable of her, I felt, to decide to build a house.

My aunt was happy to let us stay until our new house was ready. Curious, I was looking forward to seeing what new chapter our lives had in store for us. I was ready to leave our home-cum-shebeen behind. It makes one wonder, wouldn't it be a great thing to leave unpleasant memories behind every time we moved houses?

8

Astonished by a mighty storm

It seemed like an ordinary day for Elizabeth and my infant little sister, sunny and beautiful. We were busy with our mundane routine in our new home, the baby tied to her back. What happened next I cannot say but our day turned magically from being mundane to eventful. Elizabeth suffered from a serious phobia for bad weather. Any flash of lightning or thunder sent her diving for blankets. Whether it was thunder or lightning or heavy rain, her instinctive reaction was to cover with a thick blanket anything and everything that looked like a mirror. She was also superstitious. It couldn't be a black or a red blanket. It was the most hilarious thing for me to see her tip-toeing in slow motion towards the mirror. You could tell when she was getting nearer to the mirror or TV when you saw her going down in slow motion onto her elbows and knees, creeping forward in mindless terror, her legs caught up in the blankets. She'd be looking all around her, at the walls and windows, in fear for the next flash. Her face appeared less frozen than constipated—how in terror and torment she was! Storms were her nemesis. And here they come out of nowhere.

A small flicker of lightning sent her scrambling. Her next move was to hide under the nearest table, caught between covering her eyes and covering her ears. With a chubby baby on her back, you'd think she'd have acted differently but I guess there's no acting differently when you're functioning on auto-pilot. The lightning this day was like nothing we had seen. It was as if heaven and hell opened up and one or the other would swallow us. It landed like God Himself, from window to window, and there was Elizabeth inside the wardrobe with the baby still on her back. There I stood in the middle of the room, rooted to the spot, bewildered between her screams and the thunder. It seemed like a futile exercise to me, screaming against thunder.

The hail was hammering loudly on the tin roof before it was torn off entirely. And then to release a flood inside, from where I don't know, or how. And the howling wind, and the waves, like a ship at sea, fishing her out from the closet. There was no abandoning ship, no way through the windows. She had no choice now but to face her demons. If it was years of pain or tears of rain, who could tell?

Elizabeth? We both stood there helplessly, holding hands—not for support but to maintain balance. It all felt so surreal, it was a one-of-a-kind storm. As brave as I wanted to be, I was overwhelmed by the otherworldly nature of the elements. The water was up to my neck now and was whirling around her waist. I was trying to help shield my sister as she took her from her back. Still, she was in her zombie world. The way she began wading around the room irrationally like she was lost. She stumbled over something and momentarily lost her balance. She was hysterical. The look on her face was not the fear of lightning but of dying. She was murmuring and mumbling aimlessly, whether she was confessing her sordid sins, or begging for a second chance, we can never know. Just like we can never know if she was shivering from the cold or dread. Then the strangest thing happened, as quickly as the storm was unleashed upon us, it subsided. In a matter of seconds, it died down. As if it was just a storm in a teacup. Stranger things have happened in Tarkastad. Our neighbours who had just moved in came running to our rescue. I was just over four years old but I still remember the sense of relief being taken up and taken out and taken to their home. It was only then that I started shivering and shaking and going into reaction. I wept like a child should weep—refusing to be comforted. Cuddled up like a silkworm in my blanket my only thought was *I came so close to drowning.* One of their granddaughters, two years older than I, shared her wardrobe with me. They quickly prepared the coal stove for us and gave us something to eat. I remember that generous act of kindness from people whose names we didn't even know. All we knew is that they were retired farm workers, looking to raise five grandchildren in a suitable environment—hardly the environment they had in mind, no doubt, with storms blowing up out of nowhere.

Five minutes later the sun was out again. It was like it had never happened, just a nasty joke played on us by a prankster. It was now past noon, people were out and about on the streets with summer tops and sunglasses. There sat my step-father outside his new shebeen, watching us from a distance. There was no obstruction to his line of sight. He had seen everything and done nothing. Instead, he enjoyed our destruction. We slept at our new neighbours that night. First thing, the next morning, Elizabeth and I took a five-minute walk to him. We knocked for another five minutes, refusing to leave. Eventually, he opened the door but in slow motion. There he appeared in the light, his massive beer belly almost—but not quite—hiding his privates. Seeing me he turned quickly, hoping for what? That I hadn't seen him? And the image wouldn't register? While she began with her begging to be let in, I began to process the reality. I couldn't believe he could be so selfish and ruthless. I quickly became annoyed with her for even wanting to stay after he had made his priorities clear. Her begging didn't exactly get her anywhere. The mystery mistress was undoubtedly there to stay.

At last, she turned around like a spurned dog, tail between her legs. It was from that moment on that I practised the principle of self-respect and started building fortified walls around myself. This is one of the reasons I have always been labelled a proud, deep, fussy, cheeky and arrogant child.

From a very young age, I learned that you need to know and accept when you're not wanted. Be courageous enough to walk away with your dignity intact. Soon Elizabeth was to discover that her husband was just like the foolish man who built his house on the sand. As the self-appointed project manager, he had used inferior building materials and amateur bricklayers to build our home. And no remorse from him either, nor intention to rebuild. The storm that enveloped our house that day was the storm that would envelop my life. If what happened there was natural or not, I only know I survived. And that had to mean something. Against my enemy, just over the age of four, I had no weapon. But no weapon he had would prosper either.

9

A devilish angel

No doubt you've heard the writers, Jodi Picoult and Mitch Albom say "the best place to cry is in a mother's arms" or "when you look into your mother's eyes, you know that is the purest love you can find." If it was not for the credibility of these writers I would have refuted such statements off hand. One thing I can tell you about myself, I loved spending time in my head as a child—a trait that would later be inherited by my future self. It is where the most powerful conversations take place in my world, and it is where innovation is birthed, and where provoking questions arise. It wasn't until my little sister grew older that I started picking up preferential treatment towards her and subtle hatred towards me. Little did I know that subtle would evolve into blatant over time.

What this taught me as a child was: the source of a mother's love can be the source of hatred also. I wish I could tell you how it feels to cry in a mother's arms. I wish I could have seen love in my mother's eyes instead of the opposite. The idea of the warmth of a mother, the idea of how a mother's love knows neither depth nor height, remained a mystery to me. Years went by as I watched other children celebrating their mothers on Mother's Day—a day that has always been just like any other day for some of us. Somehow I couldn't ignore all that pain, the pain of rejection, of being hated by Mama when I could see she could give that warm, intimate and affectionate love to another child. She continued to bond with my little sister and gave her the love that I suspect those writers must have experienced as children—a love incomprehensible to me.

Experts in this field will say, predictably enough, that a mother's love plays an integral part in a child's emotional and cognitive development. Emotional deprivation is compared to vitamin deprivation by some professionals. In this light, I was almost convinced that Mama was pure evil. As I grew older I grew more and more conflicted as she continued to show up for others like my little brother when he was born. She was so proud to be a mother again—she seemed the happiest I had ever seen her. This bittersweet experience opened my eyes to a whole new world—a world of maturing way ahead of my time. This is where I discovered there can be a devil and an angel at the same time in one person. She could be an unkind, uncaring, uncompassionate devil in my eyes but in my eyes also a tenacious, tender and thoughtful mother to my siblings. To see her one way and see her another way with the same pair of eyes is what I call conflicting. Consequently, my little sister and brother are very close to her. To my brother, she is a queen in her own right, a goddess that he would do anything to protect.

Does that make her an angel? No! Can she be classified as a devil? I think neither. I do, however, take her for a devilish angel.

So many unanswered questions, but one thing is certain: I'm no mistake. I may have felt like I was not wanted and was unloved but there is more to it than that. Doesn't it say before He formed us in the womb He knew us? Before we were born He set us apart? So what identity, what love is it we are looking for here on earth? I can relate to this text, it gave me so much freedom—a freedom I didn't know existed.

I could experience God's immeasurable love from meditating on it and letting it sink in. But it took a conscious effort to continuously unlearn the lies I had been made to believe about myself.

For the longest time, I believed I was born a mistake, the product of something, not love, not worthy of love. I believed there must be something wrong with me to be ostracized to that degree by my biological mother—who was capable of loving. I saw myself adrift in bottomless sorrow, floundering in the pain of rejection—a pain that took hold at my throat that I could not swallow or dislodge. The pain intensified with the years, in proportion to my continued rejection. Rejection is said to be derived from the Latin *rēicere,* which roughly means *to throwback.* In essence, it is a judgment of worthiness, declaring something is simply of no value. Where I'm standing, judgment is a mental process based on opinions, which means there is a thought process to it. But what if that something is us? What if we are thrown back and declared worthless? Could it be those feelings of worthlessness in our childhood have a way of haunting us and showing up in our adulthood?

I had to channel these strong emotions somewhere. I chose to channel them into my books. I didn't excel at school because I loved my books (quite frankly, I hated them) but they were my escape zone, my place of comfort, the only way I could convince myself, and others, and dispel the notion of my unworthiness. From Sub A right through Matric I was always the youngest in class and the smartest. In extra classes, I was the one to tutor my classmates under the supervision of a class teacher. I was not only the smartest in my grade but the smartest in my school. I was "Mrs. Smarty Pants" as my seven-year-old son would call it. It felt so good to be important and worthy but for how long? I still had to go back every day to face my reality: no matter what I did, I was never good enough for Elizabeth. When I would come back with 90% from a test while the next best was 65% she would never congratulate me but would say in a disappointed voice "where is the other 10%?" When I came with 100% she'd say "shame". As if I could have done better. Here is a fact about rejection: as invisible as it is, it is invincible. The sting is long-lasting and long-reaching over years—more so when the rejection is ongoing. I had always wondered why it hurt physically until I discovered there is a part of our brain that becomes activated when we experience rejection. And it becomes activated too when we experience physical pain.

The emotional pain elicited by rejection is inevitably bound to have the same physical pain, they say. Rejection is vicious and venomous, it will eat you up and kill you from the inside without regard for your attempt to camouflage it with academic accolades, career success, marriage and children and material wealth. There is just no social status lofty enough to deliver you from it. And no amount of professional help that can acquit you either—I've been down that road. It had to take heart surgery first, a deliberate looking inward, above empty utterances. It was when I stopped climbing the corporate ladder to prove my worth that it dawned on me I was looking for external validation—a validation that quickly faded with every promotion. There was no doubled salary or lucrative performance bonus to satisfy me on my way to self-discovery. I recall the excitement of a seat at the boardroom table, "Mrs. Smarty Pants" at 25 was already part of a senior management team for a multi-million euro corporation serving 22 countries across the globe. Neither the praise I was showered with nor the red-carpet treatment nor the elite networks I created over this period satiated my longing. It wasn't until I discovered my inner sense of worth and my validation inside myself that I broke free from this vicious bondage and spat out the venomous poison of rejection that not only stole my childhood but hijacked my career and almost destroyed the one thing I value above any other: not marriage, but what comes with being married. It is at this stage that I had a full comprehension of Mark Amend's saying "rejection doesn't mean you aren't good enough; it means the other person failed to notice what you have to offer." What I can take away from this chapter of my life is, you don't choose to be rejected but you choose to be self-rejected. Know the difference. So stop seeking external validation from people who aren't even valid to begin with!

III

Part Three

Repercussions of religious hypocrisy

10

Concealed in a perfect masquerade

It was out of the blue when my parents decided to accept Jesus as their Lord and Saviour and took up church membership at Assemblies of God. I guess it was a perfect masquerade for them, to allow them to live their lie. It was the perfect platform for them to escape their reality. It gave them a channel to teleport to a world they wished to travel to. Church made them feel healed and whole—it represented a life they wished they had while giving them a sense of belonging. It was interesting to see the transformation take place as they put on their masks for church.

My step-father transformed from vicious beast to vulnerable cry baby—the first to run for the altar call and the last to leave. He was that guy, that guy to interrupt the preacher by crying bitterly throughout every sermon—you'd have thought he was sorry or genuinely repenting.

"Help us Lord" were his famous last words while weeping—to the Lord apparently—both hands lifted to heaven. No pastor was not moved by this soul who was always ready to repent. As a result, they gravitated towards him, encouraging him, loving him for setting an example for men to weep openly at church.

He had everyone eating from the palm of his hand when he decided to "burn his Calvary." That was the term used at Assemblies of God for any ungodly thing a church member had indulged in formerly.

It was not enough that you had to be half-drowned through baptism, you had to be half-burned as well. Which makes me wonder how close the ritual was to other ritualistic traditions. Old Testament law offered sacrifices in various ways—all symbolic of our own lives being substituted with the life of another. God, apparently, could be appeased by these offerings and His wrath diverted. But He would have preferred it, no doubt if an offering was not necessary in the first place. And we lived our lives as an offering anyway, by our own free will. But that was not to be and today it is no different. We bring everything but ourselves to the cross and expect God to be happy about it.

Drink was his life so that's what he brought—all his shebeen stock—worth a fortune—and burned his Calvary. I can imagine how many church members were anywhere near thinking about Calvary that day if the choice was between Jesus and the alcohol going up in flames. Either way, they applauded him for such a magnificent gesture. Here was a man with his heart in the right place.

His Oscar performance made him immediately popular—he quickly climbed up the ranks to bag the responsibilities of an ordained Elder. He was born for this kind of work.

Christianity was right up his street. You could have been going to church your whole life, been born into the church, you stood no chance against him. It all started with small tasks, from a closing prayer to an opening prayer. Before you knew it he had the church keys, which meant he was trusted to be the first and the last to leave—and boy, he didn't disappoint.

He also got trusted with church money which just shows you.

Who was that other one trusted with the church money in the Bible?

Back in the days, they used to keep hard cash in a smallish silver trunk they banked periodically. To think a man who loved money so much could be entrusted with money remains one of the magic tricks I have never seen equalled. I have no idea why they entrusted money with Judas and no idea why they entrusted it with my step-father. Eventually, he was trusted with casting out demons and by this stage, you can be forgiven for throwing this book out the window. If it wasn't for the fact that I find it funny and that it happened, I would be throwing it out the window myself. To try and describe to you how the wrestling match played out and how the stars of the show played their part, well... I will leave it for the professionals. If you've seen them in the ring you will know what I mean.

Our Elder was the champ. He'd have those allegedly demonic possessed by the collar and by the ankle and by any other thing they had and send them one by one over the ropes. As for this church, and this elder, well... there was no end to it now he was started. Out of the blue? It got worse and worse. How was I to reconcile the new creation with what I had come to know and witness? I think it is worse when someone bad through and through pretends now to be good. And presents you now as the bad guy. It was not enough to think he felt justified in treating me the way he did all along but for him to suddenly see me now as the heathen was beyond me. So I must be his burning cross, his burning Calvary, seeing as I was now the sin in his life and I must be crucified. I wonder about Jesus looking down from the cross here.

From where I stood I saw the most despicable man while the rest of the church saw only the holiest and most anointed. He had them all fooled then and he has them all fooled today. I can't pinpoint where exactly, or when, my perception of the church changed.

It may have stood for something, represented something, maybe had something to offer, before. But this stood for nothing, represented nothing and had nothing to offer. To say it made me sick to my stomach doesn't say much.

I turned from being open at least to the idea of God to being actively hateful. If this was God I wanted no part of God. If these were Christians I wanted no part in Christianity. And if this was Christ and if this was what Christ preached, I wanted no part in Christ either. What love of God? What God of love? Quite frankly, I hated them all and hated the religion that was doing this to me.

My hatred deepened with their efforts to live up to church expectations—a form of bondage that would have them spend their last money on the church and sometimes leave us with no food at home just to keep the brownie points coming. Who the Son sets free is free indeed—but here was our church in serious bondage.

The same church that was meant to bring them closer to Christ drove them farther from Him. Then our beloved Elder started stealing Elizabeth's tithes and bringing them to the priest as his. It was more important to him, I suppose, that he impressed the church. Than to impress Elizabeth. Or God for that matter. Every time the church had a conference or seminar out of town the Anointed One would volunteer to fund the trip for the whole congregation.

I concede, spending his money this way was better than spending it on mistresses, but he could not stop there either. Any money that was not church money was his money. It must all go to church, every cent, no matter whose it was or what it was for. It was like he was buying God off or something, paying for his sins, but with our money.

The last straw was years later him taking every last cent that Elizabeth had saved up for my Matric ball outfit and giving that away too. I wasn't aware of this until the day my classmates and I were meant to go shopping. In Tarkastad there were no shops but we had Queenstown at least, 60 kilometres away. One of my classmates— Korah—suggested I go with them anyway, just for fun. We were close, we had been part of an elite study group at school of which I was the leader.

She had always had a soft spot for me and this day, when I needed it most, she paid my way. Korah was three years older than I was and way mature for her age. In a loveless world, her love was real. She'd relax my hair free of charge and be one of the first classmates to give me *hammy downs* (hand-me-downs) when I needed them. And no, I never asked her for any of these things. On the chilly winter days, she would offer me one of her extra school wind breakers. I'm not sure how you would define love at that age but it must have something to do with someone shielding you against the cold. Like the light of day on a miserable night and the sun popping up over the mountain with the whole town in shadow.

The shopping spree had been planned way ahead of time—about eight months before as I remember—but our beloved Elder had made plans of his own—plans that did not include us but did include the money for my Matric ball outfit. Money, I have come to appreciate, is no big deal, but back then it most certainly was. And I took it personally, as I should—perhaps as he had intended—using it rather to fund his trip as a self-appointed church delegate to Henley on Klip, another obscure outpost of Christianity on the other side of the world. Elizabeth, out of fear of being made a laughing stock, went to a loan shark that afternoon to borrow the money that had been taken away from her—this time in the name of the Lords' work.

She had discovered that all my classmates were going, including the ones that were dependent on social grants. The embarrassment of a social worker not being able to afford a Matric ball outfit bothered her more than any other thing. She was not doing it out of love, or for me, but her. I just happened to be a lucky beneficiary.

I woke up early the next morning to get back to Queenstown to pay for the clothes I had picked the previous day and hopefully make it back in time for the ball at 10:00 am. Hitch-hiking back I found myself on the back of a logistics truck transporting a herd of sheep. I found myself counting sheep, not to go to sleep but to stay awake. What was I doing here among the sheep? Was I the black one? To be punished this way? I didn't care. It was either that or forget about the Matric ball.

Elizabeth had worked from when she was pregnant with me but she had never seen her payday. On payday, he would get all suited up and wait for her to come home over lunch. He'd demand to see her payslip and hold his big fat hands out to receive her entire salary. He would reconcile what he had in his hand with the figures on her payslip, taking into account the fish and chips she had bought for lunch—a treat she religiously adhered to every payday. I wonder if that is not why I love fried fish now still. And if that is not the only thing I got out of it. And maybe her too. But she had to produce the cash receipts and if there was a 5c short he would go for her throat. R5 short was a black eye. This was the story of her life—a life I believe she chose. Come Fathers Day he was asked to "share the Word". Imagine what honour it would be for any of us to do so. But for him it was an opportunity to ramble on from the pulpit and bragging about the goodness of the Lord for giving him such a romantic and submissive wife. I'm not sure, perhaps for her a black eye was romantic. Or for him it was. He stuck his arm out to show them a chunky gold wristwatch he had bought himself the previous day using Elizabeth's hard-earned money—claiming it was a gift from her. He praised the Lord for his deliverance, saying that he now uses a handkerchief on his wife instead of fists—the same fists he rained on her as we left for church that morning.

At this point the church was pure torture for me. If a little stick figure could be a time bomb it was me—up to my limit with the lies and the pretence.

Tic tic tic you can hear it. *Tic tic* ticking away.

How many times was I tempted to go on stage when they were forcing testimonies out of us? How much better for them that I didn't. I wasn't planning to testify to any wondrous works of the Dear Lord but to reveal the long-overdue truth—like how wondrous it was up to now that the Dear Lord had not blasted them out of the building—but I couldn't! And my inner clock just carried on *tic tic* ticking. I didn't know where to start and I was too full of rage and resentment. It was nothing but rage and resentment that silenced me. I was suffocating and choking in it—in my home town, in my hell home, and my church alike.

The two places that are said to be the safest places were the places providing only trauma for me.

Revival they are always praying for, revival of what? Basic human compassion and dignity? A bit of honesty perhaps? And a bit of truthfulness, even the tiniest grain, to make the world palatable?

My worst church memory was during a church revival. A friend of mine had missed the first part of the sermon and wanted to catch up. She leaned over my shoulder to ask where the reading was from. Watchful against getting myself into the Elder's bad books, I gently took her Bible and turned where we were reading. Our Sunday School teacher, Pinky—bored out of her skull no doubt—was giving us thee look. As if we were up to no good. On our way home after the service the Elder confronted me for tainting the family name. *We had a name?* I was asking myself. *For what? Hypocrisy?* "By causing a scene during the sermon" he said. Not that he had seen anything but that was our snitch Sunday School teacher reporting to the parents just like Sunday School teachers should do. She had asked him—not me—to ask me to stay away from my friend because she was "bad news". As if I had not grown up between the hammer and anvil of bad news. She was no bad news but good news rather—unless you were threatened by an open-minded young girl from Johannesburg whose recently divorced mother was far from submissive or conformist. They didn't like her and her family. They were not religious enough for them. To them, religion meant not having a mind of your own. There was nothing much I could say to defend myself besides tell what happened. I knew the truth didn't matter, he would beat me nonetheless. What I didn't know was he would go for my nose with a plank until the plank broke in half. Here was the nose thing now, like the hair thing. An obsession with my nose. He had always hated the pointyness and the straight edge unlike the others—as if this difference alone was reason enough for him to attack me. The Nose, if I may call it that, elicited a weird reaction from him every time a stranger complimented me, or the church people paid tribute to it. He would even ask me why my nose was different from the rest of the family—except everything about me was different from the rest of the family—why stop at the nose. From their light skin tones to rounded bodies to not much wit, I was as different as a stick insect is to a tortoise. But even then, The Nose was only the starting point. There was The Eyes also, and The Face. My looks tortured him in ways God only knows. I'm told I was a participant in beauty pageants as a preschooler and bagged the crown each time—something I vaguely have flashes of. Then it dawned on me! Remember his obsession with combing my hair and covering my face? I realized as I grew more eyes that it was never about me but about my beauty. He was hiding my beauty like in the parable, hiding your light under a bushel, so no one could see it—a beauty that afflicted him and provoked him and tormented him in his darkness and in his insecurities toward Elizabeth. He used to tell me from my preschool days, "you're a whore just like your mother"—not that I've seen Elizabeth whoring ever! Only hard-working! But then again, it takes one to know one right? Is there even such a thing as a whore in preschool? "Pretty" and "whore" were used interchangeably in the

Elder's vocabulary. Yes! I was pretty, probably as pretty as Elizabeth was in her youth—half of me is her after all—but my beauty was a curse to him, a daily remembrance of a mysterious pain he tried so hard to deny. I guess it's called human idiosyncrasies. And it fits perfectly well with playing the game. And wearing your mask dutifully in the masquerade.

11

Rusty steel rails

I remember being six years of age, travelling by train with my parents and my little sister to a church conference in Thaba Nchu, Free State—my little sister was barely a year old at the time. As we got to our destination, Bethulie, in the early hours of the morning, I recall the overloaded train and a stampede of people rushing to make their way through the exit without losing their belongings in the process. Before I knew it I was lying on my back surrounded by rusty steel on either side and when I looked up all I could see was more rusty steel. It turned out I was under the train! My heart seemed to stop beating as I heard the train whistle and the clank and clutter of couplings.

From there I remember the wheels in motion, vast circles of cutting steel. The distant choo was my death knell, I knew I was finished. I knew those wheels were going to make six-year-old mincemeat out of me. What puzzles me to this day is: out of the restricted options I had that moment, crying out loud was just not one of them. It's like somehow I've always known that I've been, and will be, on my own. Or perhaps like in any other moment of trauma, I was overwhelmed by feelings of numbness and dissociation. Honestly, I don't think a six-year-old would know the difference. Beneath the moving train, beneath the undercarriage, I saw Elizabeth—my mother looking right into my eyes. Her eyes said everything at that moment, her face a death mask untouched by compassion, connection or concern. Then it all happened like lightning—a strong hand pulling my arm then more hands pulling my body then even more pulling my legs.

Next thing I was out, snatched free from the wheels, blown back by the fury and noise of the maddened steel. It was as if the train was a ravenous beast and the beast had been cheated of his prey. Strangers talking in a strange tongue gathered me to the nearest bench where they fussed over me in an attempt to establish whether I had truly escaped unscathed or suffered some form of injury. At this point my parents materialised, on cue, to "politely" thank the strangers. They took over from there and we carried on with our journey as if nothing happened, business as usual.

"Are you okay baby?"

That's a natural instinctive question from a normal mother, which begs the question, was Elizabeth even normal? Yes, no manual comes with motherhood, and no experience is ever the same, granted! But what I could not comprehend, and battled with for so many years, was, how could she be so cold? Was she hoping that I would be mashed by that train so she could pretend to be this grieved mother who lost her child so tragically and had to supposedly live with the traumatized memory of watching her six-year-old daughter die so terribly?

Well, we can never know now, can we? After a couple of days, we came home again on the train, triggering the ordeal afresh. I sat there reliving my recent trauma, at the same time trying to figure out... how did I survive? Just when death was about to swallow me...

Rewinding that day, playing it back in my mind, the train slowing down, preparing to stop, Elizabeth preparing to exit from the doors. We'd witnessed commuters not being fast enough to get off and being forced to get off at the next stop and take another train back to their original destination—no announcements to warn you either, preparing you for the next station. And travelling at night also, in a region where we didn't speak the language. The best you could do was keep a lookout and be watchful for signs as they appeared and be ready at the doors when they opened. Elizabeth knew the drill, the baby on her back, rushing for the doors. I was left with my step-father to unload luggage through the window. He was taking the lighter luggage down first and handing it to me to hand to Elizabeth. Then the whistleblowing and the engine sounding as if he knew—the train driver—sensing what was about to happen. It was the whistle blow—call it what you will—the death signal, that triggered him into a panic. He knew there was no way he could make it to the exit with heavy luggage and me around him. So he picked me up and called to Elizabeth to catch me as she was done with the rest of the luggage. By now my little sister was standing next to her and she was ready with both arms to catch me. Only she approached me hesitantly, like someone weighing her options. She came close enough not to make it obvious but far enough not to catch me. And as I fell from his arms into the gap between the train and the platform she didn't scream or shout for help. Like somehow she was hoping no one had noticed I was trapped down there under the wheels.

And when our eyes locked I saw what I had not seen before: a prayer, not for a miracle, no, but my demise. *I hope you rot down there* her eyes were saying. And I'm not sure if any face ever betrayed less feeling or less concern for another living thing. It was so dark under there, so crowded with everyone going about their business, I was not meant to be noticed. If it was not my step-father hiding my face behind my hair—hoping I wouldn't be seen—then it was my mother murdering me in plain sight—hoping I would remain hidden. I know it's beyond bizarre for a daughter to accuse her mother of murder, but I have—and she did not deny it! Just like she did not have the words to defend herself. "I've never seen such a deep child" has been her only response. "God knows where you come from." I heard those words from her every time I stood up or spoke up for myself. No doubt I was a damaged child.

My childhood memories are not ordinary. I was only six but I remember the day like it was yesterday. I wish I didn't. It took me close to 25 years to have this conversation with her because a naive part of me, the little girl, wanted to believe the best—the best of her mother. Turns out I wasn't hallucinating all that hate towards me that I had been picking up. What is it that can cause a mother to resort to murdering a child that was already going through hell—a hell that she didn't sign up for?

Was I such a thorn in the flesh for her?

At 33 I still can't wrap my head around this one.

Who could? If we were talking about my vile psychopath of a step-father, I would understand. It's like she saw the opportunity as he presented me out the window—a living sacrifice. And in the heat of the moment, with noise all around, people all over, she took the opportunity. That's the moment of truth, the reality for me, the little window, the portal by which I could see for that instant into the abyss that was my mother's soul.

No man had been there.

No God either.

For the universe it was a closed book, and still is. And later, when she came to collect me again, take me out from the hands of strangers, who had rescued me, and comforted me, I remembered again those eyes. The disappointment that I had survived. She couldn't hide it, not even for PR purposes.

So close she was thinking, as I was.

So close.

So many forces at play in the world. So many powers at work. Flesh and blood, heart and mind, soul and spirit. I wonder what word it was, or what action, that intervened that day. I feel like I literally witnessed what God means in Isaiah 59:1 when He says, *"Behold, the Lord's hand is not shortened, That it cannot save; Nor His ear heavy, That it cannot hear."* It's scary to see how relevant the Bible can be, in one's day-to-day life. Life was to show me more and today I can testify that a thousand may fall at my side and ten thousand at my right hand, but still, *it will not come nigh me.* And indeed, *"He gives his angels charge over thee, to keep thee in all thy ways. They shall bear thee up in their hands, lest thou dash thy foot against a stone."*

12

Falsely accused

It was customary at Assemblies of God to have a fundraiser every first Sunday of the month called "Assemblies Business". Essentially the church would get divided into small groups and compete against one another over a series of rounds before the preaching and "getting drunk in the Holy Ghost." The group to raise the highest amount would be given a championship title while all the money would be kept for the House of the Lord. The stingy folks would make sure they teamed up with the ones with deep pockets who didn't mind to keep going to the pulpit to redeem or maintain their lead. Regardless of the good intention of Assemblies Business it was now turned into a recreational activity and a platform to flex one's financial muscle—something that would undoubtedly stir the zeal of our Lord to throw tables around, but hey, who am I to talk?

The Elder was one of the flexors while Elizabeth was a tag-along, making her a flexor by default. For this reason, then, I assume, we were sent to a loan shark not far from our house by our mother. Lending from a shark, no doubt, to give to the Lord. And you ask why around this time I was having problems with the Lord.

My sister and I had been up early and were ready for Sunday School and upholding the family name. We'd need to be the first to arrive which meant most of the time sitting in a huge, chilly, empty church like two baby ghosts after earning more browny points for our parents by dusting off chairs.

Our snitch Sunday School teacher would show up for the service five minutes before 10:00 while pretending to the rest of the folks that she had been spooking and haunting the church alongside us. It seemed like deception was the name of the game—no wonder my parents felt like they belonged, finally! The loan shark was not interested in lending Elizabeth any money. "I'm not interested in anything to do with your mother," she said, glaring at us. It didn't seem like her reasons were related to money but rather a "beef" they had at the clinic.

Elizabeth's passion for her job came at the cost of making enemies along the way—the loan shark's brother and mother had applied for a social grant which Elizabeth had to motivate for as the allocated social worker. My guess is she must have refused one of the applications, or both.

As we ran back home I decided not to report the facts as I knew they would be followed by an interrogation that we had no answers for.

"She doesn't have the money!" I said to Elizabeth as I passed through the kitchen to grab my pocket Bible in the room for Sunday School.

It was me going through the motions just like any other day but as I stepped back into the kitchen I was confronted with the beast and his belt—wet still from the bath.

He came at me like a hurricane with hurricane force behind him. I wished for the floors to open up and swallow me. The rage and force and fury of his charge—and the unexpectedness of it—caught me totally off guard. He had me by the throat now with his face up in my face and his eyes and nose bulging and his devilish breath blasting me from hell. "You are the cheekiest child I know!" he blasted at me, flinging me down. Then he turned his belt around so the buckle dragged on the floor. "Today you will taste my buckle," he said, his words falling like a death sentence. "I think that's what you need. I've been very lenient on you." Then a kind of animal whooping, as if to gather more power.

"You will know me today," he said and his favourite form of exercise began, only different from the others because of the metal buckle. So it started and continued for as long as his strength lasted, landing the buckle over my legs and thighs and not stopping even when I was bleeding.

I begged and begged for forgiveness like Elizabeth would—for doing nothing wrong—serving only to justify his actions and encourage him further.

Begging forgiveness during a workout session was like adding fuel to the flames—you were asking him to go harder and stronger. He would go from medium pace to no holds barred, open gates, anything goes, a bull in a china shop—the china shop being me.

I still vividly recall the confusion I felt throughout the ordeal. I had no idea what it was I had done wrong or what the fury was about.

The charge

the accusation

the reason, was denied me. It would be delivered as an afterthought when he had spent his rage. The exhaustion was the only thing that could stop him. But the hurricane was not yet done. Spent, perhaps, but not done.

As if the murderous attack on me was but foreplay he now ripped off the orange wraparound skirt that I had put on for church that morning—which sent me peeing on myself immediately and my knees shaking uncontrollably.

I was convinced that he was about to rape me—I was old enough now to know what that was. My thoughts were not exactly unfounded—he had it tried before, one afternoon after school as I was changing into my "work" clothes. I had a job waiting for me at the clay pit.

He had called me into their room and acted all weird, muttering to himself and pacing the room like a caged animal, working himself up for the deed. He reached for his belt buckle and I wondered what was it now I had done. But he slipped the belt off and threw it in the corner. Then he zipped down his bottle-green pants and began fumbling at his fly.

It didn't need a social worker to know what was about to go down. I often think about this. How a girl should react. What she should do. When she is approached this way by someone she knows. Alone, no one around, no one to come to her rescue. A man far bigger and stronger than you. And you are a girl. With nothing but your sense of helplessness and desperation. But to think is not an option when you are in the situation. So you do what you can do. And you scream. Looking back it was all I had. God knows enough women have screamed in that place where I was and nobody came to help. But our big man was a coward through and through and a hypocrite. The image he projected of being a churchman was too important to him—more important than his sexual urge or his desire to overpower and destroy a creature he detested.

"Bloody whore!" he yelled as he backed off from me, zipping up his pants. "You're such a filthy bloody whore! Bitch!" he went on.

"That's why your mind was ahead of me!" So everything he was, he was now calling me. That's typical. Shame others so you need not feel shame. Rather kill myself I said, but wouldn't that be falling into the trap? That same day, the same day we had gone to church as a Happy Family, the same day he preached a storm and made jokes in the pulpit, I told myself I would rather die than let the man I abhorred more than anything in existence penetrate me.

Sunday was my day it seems. I'm seeing a pattern here of going to church and being savagely attacked by devils. I'm wondering if there is a connection. Or if they are the same thing. Either way, Sunday was never a day of rest for me but rather a day of torment. Whatever hell is waiting for us I cannot imagine it being worse than this.

Back to my hurricane.

Hurricane Sunday. *I'm naked again. He'll finish now what he started before. What his son failed to go through before.* My trauma was with me still and on top of the trauma was the ultimate fear: rape. But again, the churchman took charge of the flesh man. Suddenly it was getting ready for church rather, church is more important. *Whatever state you are in, get ready. We can't be late. You've made us late as it is.* This must have been his thinking as he came back from our room with a powder blue silky ankle-length skirt that he flung in my face. "You better cover your bloody black legs," he said. "And next time I send you for something, report back to me, not your mother."

There now was the little moment of madness that would drive anyone else insane. I was to report to him, not to my mother? But my mother had sent us! I stood there in excruciating pain, emotionally wrecked, trying to process the facts. It was more than an assault on my body but on my mind and my psyche and my spirit. It was official now, my devil step-father needed no excuse, no reason, to do as he pleased with me. He could make up anything he liked and make out like it had been the law since Adam.

He owned me is what he was saying. The message was loud and clear. And if he felt like belting me to shreds, he would. Who was going to do anything about it? You can say what you like about it, you man of the court, you lawman, you social worker. Domestic violence? Corporal punishment? I'm no judge but I know what a human being is. And that was not human, what had just happened. He was borderline evil and psychotic. His nostrils were puffed up, he heaved in and out with every sentence, his heart straining to keep up with his breathing.

"You have no regard for me," he said. "I've been watching you." He had no regard for himself he meant to say. And I was watching him. Swaying like a high tree above me, giddy with intoxication. For him, it was over. The tornado had moved on. But he couldn't leave it there. Not before laying the final stroke. "You better give your best smile at church today. And don't you dare be late for Sunday School." Sunday School. Yes. So that was what this was all about. In a crucifixion of pain, in a psychological state beyond description, I looked down. I was a mess of blood and bruises and lacerations. My body, after all, was swollen and black. I had assumed he was alluding to my skin colour, not the black bloody marks from his buckle.

I noticed as I began cleaning myself a dripping of blood that I couldn't trace to anything on me till I stood before the mirror and turned around slowly and saw the hole in my left thigh beneath my buttock. His belt buckle had taken a chunk of flesh, a bit of me, out of me! *I must be mad* I thought. *I must be seeing things. My eyes must be playing tricks on me.* And you may well ask where Elizabeth was up to now. Hiding in her room along with my little sister that had gone with me to the loan shark. And no explanation there as to why she did not get punished. And here we have hypocrisy at last at its worst, its demonic worst, because this is my mother we were talking about. A Social Worker to everyone outside, except for me, her own child, under her roof. "Mama" I called from our room and she came, the Responsible Social Worker now, to attend to the damage. After the damage was done. And the perpetrator was safely gone and no danger to her. And he having unleashed the storm on me. And now, the crocodile tears from Elizabeth. Or if they were genuine tears, who can tell? And who was she crying for exactly? She was good at dressing wounds, no doubt, even if they were the wounds of her own making. But now the tears, tears of what, I don't care. I used the opportunity to ask her why she didn't stand up for the truth. She knew she was the one who sent us, not him. The same way my little sister knew and chose to keep quiet. I could accept she would never protect me nor stand up for me but I had never envisioned my own mother saying nothing while I was falsely accused.

Somehow there was this pathetic belief in Elizabeth still, and the truth. The two must go together or there could be neither. The injustice of it and the excuse he used and the reasoning and the mad logic was unbearable on top of the load I was already carrying. What hell was this now on top of the hell I was in? What bloody madness?

The insanity of my world was never more excruciatingly evident than here in our room that day in the hands of a weeping mother. Reason has no place here. Rational thought, logic. All that we call sanity was insanity here, all that was rational was crazy. Anybody could do anything and nobody would be held accountable for it. It was that kind of whirlwind, a mental whirlwind, the hurricane I was picked up in. And here I was expecting her to stand up for the truth, if not for the Department of Social Development and the Child Welfare Unit she represented so well in our rotten community. She sold me out! She sold my body and soul out! She sold herself out and that seems to me to be the most insane part of it all. As usual, she replied with a church hymn. *"How great thou art..."* etc..Bruised and battered. Dripping with blood. I could barely move from one point to the next inside the house, the pain from the friction between my thighs was unbearable. God knows how I got to church that day or how I sat on my bruised and bloodied flesh for three hours. The service alone was torment enough but listening to the hypocrites was torturous.

As I say, it was bad luck for me on Sundays. Or the devil was out and about more than usual, in the name of God. Sunday seems to be the day most people remember with joy. I remember them only with unutterable despair. It was on a Sunday when we came back from church one day to a surprise visitor—my step-brother with his PhD. in house burglary and armed robbery. He had made his way inside the most secure house in the neighbourhood. The paranoid ex-cop with all his security keys had still not managed to keep his estranged son from finding a way in without forcing an entrance. He stayed a couple of days, coming in and out as he pleased—that's how Emily raised him—Emily his grandmother—"our" grandmother. He was staying with Emily from the minute his mother died and was treated like a grieving child ever since. His appalling behaviour was perennially excused and he got away with whatever he wanted—including Emily's social grant. Then he would beat her up on top of it for good measure, just like the Bible says—pressed down, shaken together, and running over. What's this about an apple not falling far from the tree? The more he beat up Emily, the more she treated him like the man of the house. There was something seriously twisted about the women in my childhood—the way they embraced domestic violence and treated it as a symbol of love puzzled me. It was almost like a kind of foreplay. A woman couldn't love her man unless he loved her this way. And he couldn't be aroused unless he did so. The day he left our house and was never seen again was the day he stole what was inside the little silver trunk that belonged to the District Assembly of the Assemblies of God and was due to be banked at the end of that month. The only reason we still had it at that time was the great Elder himself. Entrusted with the box he had used some of it for his personal use and was waiting for Elizabeth's payday to refund it. No surprises here for anyone still with us by now. I'll spare you the details but you can imagine what hell landed on me again for not babysitting a grown man in his step-father's house. Again, some fabricated reason that had nothing to do with anything I had ever heard of before, somehow related to money. It was now my fault he stole the money—according to our psychotic step-father I was supposed to follow him around the house and watch his every move. While in survival mode I was trying my best to stay away from him in case he was here to finish what he had started back then when he laid me on the couch and pulled my panties off. Again my little sister was standing by but no word of correction or scolding in that direction, no. As for the assaults, she seemed to have caught up with the rules of engagement and capitalized accordingly—knowing what the outcome would be. It would have been nice to have a sister to care for and to care for me but it was not to be. I still have my scar where the chunk of flesh was torn out by the belt buckle. My children call it my birthmark and I don't tell them any different. I think often of the nail-scarred hands in this case and what His back must have looked like afterwards. The One who knew no sin, but was made sin for us. That we might become the righteousness of God.

13

Sharp-eyed old hag

One of the things I learned from my husband is, the people that hurt us and walk around as if nothing happened are just pretending. He has always been convinced that come the midnight hour, when there's no one to impress or perform for, their conscience catches up with them. They might be pretending not to be bothered by their ugly deeds, but the truth is, deep down they're haunted. I have always wondered if there were any exceptions to this belief because with my step-father he acted like he was not bothered at all by his deeds. The only thing he cared for was being caught for who and what he was. His reputation was everything and Elizabeth seemed to have jumped on the bandwagon.

To ensure that he controlled the intel and narrative—like any Public Relations specialist—I had to account for every conversation I'd had every day. I'd have to give details of who I'd bumped into on my way to the shop, what they said, and how I responded, including how long the conversations had lasted. The same went for the shop owners who personally knew my parents—failure to comply with this daily ritual resulted in punishment. Such moments may seem insignificant but these were the defining moments for me.

My hatred for him was aggravated by such ludicrous behaviour. These are the points where I felt less human and more of an object—an object that he had sole rights to.

I can't remember why I landed up at the clinic that particular day—my visits to Elizabeth were restricted. Her colleague needed someone to send to the shop for bread. She asked Elizabeth if she could send me and I was back from the shop with the bread before she could return to her work inside the clinic—a matter of minutes.

One, she could not believe her eyes.

Two, she was not impressed.

Three, it was too good to be true.

Rhoda was her name, an old hag you could say, the longest standing employee at the clinic and due for retirement soon. Rhoda was no angel and everyone knew it. She had no use for a mask or pretending to be St Rhoda, even though her husband owned a church and was an Archbishop. She had a reputation to uphold in society but from where I stood she was not defined by society's standards. She had a tough exterior and a rough demeanour and a tongue not shy to let fly from across the street. There was nothing dignified about her, no logical reason to look up to her or give her the respect she enjoyed in the community. It was only that mouth and that tongue and that fearlessness. They feared her and her superiors feared her and that's all there was to it.

She was contractually hired as a cleaner but she didn't care much for her job description.

Jack-of-all-trades was more in her line, inventing her job description. She knew how to dispense medicine, dress wounds and how to lead the health education sessions, which was Elizabeth's job, and she only made tea for the colleagues she got along with. In short, Rhoda was the boss! This day she called Elizabeth aside and wanted to know if I wasn't being abused at home. Because what I had done was virtually impossible. What did my mother do? I sometimes wonder. If there was a guilty look or a furtive glance. A face drained of colour or a face betraying guilt or fear or even a tiny bit of remorse, even for a second. If maybe a hymn was her only answer to the sharp-eyed hag. *"EVIL me oh thou great Jehovah..."* What did she do? What any mentally unstable mother would do. Report me to Head Office.

Now I must be abused again for acting suspiciously. For purposely promoting the idea I was being abused. By running so fast and getting back so quickly. "Spoiled brat! Just looking for attention again!" So here I was, doing what my evil step-father had trained me to do: the unimaginable. Flying like the devil to get there and back again. But now it was held against me. As if it was my fault.

I have to commend the old hag, her sharp eyes spotted a unique creature, the product of intense training under extreme pressure. From a very young age, this demon I had called a father would send me to the shop and spit on the ground and instruct me to be back before his spit dried out. Think about that. Spit as you spit in contempt. Spit as you spit at your enemy's feet. Spit as you spit in the face of Christ.

I failed the test several times and paid for it with serious assaults and stoning with rocks until I could come back with the spit still not dried out. Then he would send me farther to shops farther away and I was back to the drawing board until I got it right again. I say it in a sentence like that but try living it out from day to day, year in, year out.

A sentence seems such a short thing really in context to reality. Did none of the neighbours notice?

Me sprinting like the devil was at my heels? Indeed he was, and he was fast. As heavy and fat and bulging as he was—with legs as short as his belly was fat—he was as quick as quick could be, there was no outrunning him.

And then he would stone me along the way like a dog—like nothing human at all—in the name of motivating a cheeky child. It was a nightmare I was living in and to think about it now and to write about it is to be in the nightmare still.

There was nothing you could do to appease him.

Nothing you could do to meet the mark. Meet it and he would set the mark higher again.

All the while laughing at me and feeling powerful no doubt. So he started sending me to town, a new game altogether. Instead of spitting once, he'd do it three times, four times, five times, depending on the mood. I'd have to run from the township to town—3 km—and from town back to the township—3 km—before the spit dried out. This must be the reason I excelled in athletics, barefoot, outrunning the fastest runners in their running shoes.

But even then I found a way to reward myself and the psychologists no doubt will have the answer. I had to make my hell enjoyable rather than endurable. I had to find a way to motivate myself, other than being stoned like a stray dog. I had to have something to look forward to, something to provide an incentive.

To somehow deny the beast and deny the devil and deny the reality even. I would create my reality apart from his.

Mischief was always my first love, my instinctive reflex action to anything needing solutions. It became a stimulant for me like any drug, taking my mind off my trauma. The idea of doing something scary and yet remaining fearless was what gave me my rush. Did I care that it came at a detrimental cost to someone else? Not a chance!

I soon recruited two of my athlete friends to join me along my route to town and back. The route would include a stop at a local cafe that sold the best biltong there is in the Karoo. Needless to say, we shipped more biltong out from that shop than the owner could ship in and when we were busted one day it was scary and exhilarating at the same time with the police van on our tails and us relying solely on fast footwork and thinking on your toes. You'd think after that we'd stop but it doesn't work that way. I was addicted. In the same way, you don't just stop being an alcoholic, you don't stop with mischief.

It got so bad that I would be asking my step-father if he didn't need anything in town, just so I could run the risk again. More than the biltong—that I still love—was the mischief that came with it.

You could say that in one way my step-father turned me into some kind of a criminal. But I prefer to think it was just a hunted creature turned hunter, the prey turned predator. Someone had to lose in this game and it could not forever be me.

Still, I wonder if the world still has mothers like Rhoda in our communities, in our churches and schools.

Mothers who can look and see through the windows of every tender soul. To discern between impressive and alarming.

To differentiate between a disciplined child and a programmed child.

To determine between incredible and spine-chilling. May Rhoda's magnificent soul rest in peace! Flying to the shop was in my default settings—settings that were abnormal for any child. From that moment she became a hero to me, while she was called a witch by others. Her motherly instincts made me feel understood and at that moment, that's all I needed. Suddenly I had hope that one day the truth would find a way of sticking its tongue out, its toes out, and finally its head.

There would come a day when the truth could no longer be boxed in by PR strategies and Bible texts. Her discovery on the other hand made me hate the church people for turning the other eye.

The signs of domestic abuse had always been there. You didn't even have to look hard enough, you just had to use common sense like Rhoda and be mindful. We hosted church guests regularly at home, and no ordinary guests either—a special delegation rather—six members appointed to high-level sensitive classified matters.

At Assemblies of God, they had a name for them: the DC, short for the District Committee. They were like your MI6, CIA and KGB but in a church setting.

As a select group of trusted agents, you'd have thought they'd be able to read the signs. No such luck. And here I did my part. I did what any other girl like me would do if she was in my situation and she had the courage and the opportunity.

I approached a younger preacher who must have been in his mid-thirties at the time—not so far out of reach for me in youth and empathy. It was then I realized how rotten our church was. I shared with him just a bit of it, the high-level abuse. In reply, he preached openly over my grievances during one of the mid-week services: "Children, obey your father and mother."

As if I had not heard it a thousand times before and could not add in the same breath: "parents, provoke not your children to wrath." There's a scripture now. But only the one you want to hear, right?

No one wants to hear about provoking your children to wrath. But we must all obey our parents for this is right, etc. "As unto the Lord." Yes, I can quote you Bible verses, I can quote you a few more, I've heard them all. But no doubt you will not want to hear the ones you have not heard before.

Then I couldn't help wondering if the DC aka M16 aka CIA aka KGB had not decided to turn a blind eye to our dysfunctional home. I was more than ever disgusted and my hatred for church and God grew even stronger.

How could a trusted guardian of the faith be so merciless to use holy scripture to advance the cruelty of parents while invalidating my pain?

What gives church leaders the right to reduce people's traumas to nothing, in the name of God?

If that is what God is all about then I will gladly pass, which I did. To attach a higher power and depict that power to be one who purposefully hurts children and stands by while they are abused by their parents is Satanic.

It is pure evil to dismiss the humanity of innocent children, to dismiss their excruciating pain, to deny their horrific experiences at the hands of their parents all in the name of honouring their parents.

God didn't create us to be abused and stay mentally depressed as a result. If anything, God hurts when we hurt. Seeing us traumatized and stay traumatized has never been part of God's will for our lives.

It took me some time to learn to stand by my truth—that I didn't have to shrink and be dismissed—that my pain mattered and didn't require any external validation to qualify it.

14

Ruminations

Introduced to Assemblies of God church from an early age, having endured a childhood there, being raised as a churchgoing person up to the time that I left home, I have some feelings about churchgoing and church life that has helped me to formulate ideas of my own. That may be the first point. Who teaches you to think for yourself?

I know only one, who spoke in parables and planted seeds instead of laying down the law. If our Teacher was an independent thinker, should we not be following in His footsteps? But no, we are taught to accept someone else must do our thinking for us. It starts at home, it progresses through school and if you are particularly lucky, like me, it ends in church. From Sunday School to Bible Study to Prayer Meeting to Church Social, all work together to complete the task of teaching you not to think for yourself. "Who the Son sets free is free indeed" is written, is it not bizarre that you need to find your freedom outside of church? Then there is the matter of taking the name in vain. Thou shalt not, it is written, but look, we do.

What does it mean? It means to take the name for no reason and no purpose. To make light of the name and to use it for other things.

To call yourself a Christian or a follower of Christ but not to follow Christ and not to be like Christ in your thoughts and actions is to take the name in vain, to steal the name, a good name, and make it a bad name. To take what does not belong to you in the first place is stealing, to go on and drag it through the mud is something else.

No one can ever teach you these things in the churches I've been to. You need to be out of it to see it.

And when you pray "lead us not into temptation but deliver us from evil" it is often the church you are praying about. Last but not least, let us talk hypocrisy. As part of the program on Sunday at Assemblies of God was a slot for electing one of the elders to pray for leaders everywhere.

The congregation would be standing and they would read from Paul's letter to Timothy: "In every place of worship, I want men to pray with holy hands lifted to God, free from anger and controversy." While on one hand, the man to pray would need to confess that his hands were holy, on the other it was the responsibility of the church to ensure that they appointed the closest thing to "holy". To my surprise, the church had no problem appointing our great Elder even after I had reported the domestic abuse.

And he gladly confessed "holy hands" without a thought for blasphemy or lightning bolts from the sky. What had his hands not been doing before then? And what would they still do?

I couldn't help but feel they were making a mockery of God. I couldn't help but wonder, was God even there? Or which God were they praying to? Either way, I wasn't surprised much about the Holy Hands charade considering how quickly they welcomed him back when he impregnated one of the trusted worship leaders—another sin that I had to pay for, only this time Elizabeth, yes! My mother was the debt collector. Somehow it was my fault that her husband was having an affair with a girl in her early twenties—perhaps because I was closer to that age than she was. It was my job, apparently, not anyone else's, not even my sister's to babysit her husband. My sister lived a charmed life, free of any responsibility. While everything that went wrong was always my fault.

On that particular Sunday Elizabeth was welcomed by the older ladies and mothers at church. They had brought out a chair for her and turned our sunny spot outside into some kind of reception area. They had been given instructions to keep her company as they broke the news to her—that her husband had eaten from the forbidden fruit and taken a mistress (at this stage they knew nothing about the pregnancy.) I wonder still about this scene and the strange reaction that followed.

Was the job given to the ladies by the elders? If so, why the ladies? Why again must the woman be given the job the man cannot do? Or is it the man's way of saying he knows he was in the wrong? It was just, you know, the man thing doing its thing again.

The picture seems to resonate with me as a picture of the church. Men doing their thing and women picking up the pieces. Then you can take it further and ask what happened to the baby? Which holy hands were now busy with the abortion since the baby miraculously vanished? He squashed it as best he could but he couldn't squash the fact that his anointed worship leader also happened to be in school still. He gladly holy handed money for a Matric ball outfit and various "sundries." When my turn came I was to go dressed in rags and be called a "spoiled brat."

When poor Elizabeth heard the news she was taken aback, which left me puzzled. It was almost as if she had forgotten at that moment that the only sin the Elder had stopped with was drinking excessively—not the cheating or abuse and violent assaults.

And now, when she needed a hymn, she suddenly didn't have one. Funny, right? Drinking remains a stumbling block for religion to this day. To focus on the popular *thou shalt not consume alcoholic beverages* commandment, which I am yet to find in my Bible, is one of the greatest misconceptions in society! The Bible is clear on drinking—Christ came eating and drinking, turning water into wine. They called him a glutton and a drunkard.

A lot of church folks would know this if they gave themselves time to question the Christian religion and read the Bible for what it is, not what they want it to be. And no, this is not me recruiting for Nederburg or AB InBev or Distell for that matter—I don't drink! But the Bible was never given for an arbitrator, or to judge who is holier than who. Drunkenness = gluttony, they're both called overindulging for a reason. Before you judge another for drinking consider your eating. The finger you point at another points back at you three times.

I'd love to see the day where topics like overeating and overspending are preached from the pulpit with the same zeal as "thou shall not drink."

Mostly the man who must "burn his Calvary" for church finds Calvary elsewhere. Rarely do we hear such things in our churches. What society has chosen to take out from the Christian religion is far from what it is truly about. Perhaps the core of the matter was never about religion but spirituality. It's time we unlearn every lie that was dressed in truth and seek the truth for ourselves.

I'm not bashing going to church but can we stop hiding behind Bible verses at our convenience? Yes, sure, the gathering of the brethren is encouraged and I appreciate that—but not when the price tag is pure blasphemy. I didn't find God in church, I found Him at home, alone, unlearning everything I was taught in those godless places—where God was meant to be.

Often I sit and imagine a time when we as Christians would stop taking things at face value but seek knowledge for ourselves instead.

I imagine a generation that will be rewarded for exercising curiosity to discover a world beyond the realm of what society expects them to subscribe to. I stand in awe at the possibilities for Christian churches abstaining from punishing broad-mindedness and curiosity.

Can you imagine a revolution in churches where leaders couldn't be bothered with ranks and titles? A leadership that will be able to tell the difference from a distance between folks with a spirit of servanthood and folks who are merely power-hungry, going to church not to feed their souls—or their shepherds for that matter—but their egos? Or perhaps they're serving "faithfully" because they're bored, they've got nothing better to do with their time, and suddenly serving in the house of the Lord makes them feel important.

Isn't that confusing sheer boredom with so-called servanthood? Serving the Lord is not confined within the four walls of a church building.

Serving the Lord is about being obsessed and determined to advance the Kingdom of God, and ensuring that God's interests are established and promoted through your life.

I may be unsure about a lot of things but there's one thing I'm sure of, I am servant of the Most High; I establish and advance His Kingdom albeit my non-existing church membership. For instance, writing this book is one of the ways I am of service to the Lord. You may ask: Asa I hear you but how do I join you in serving the Lord? Well....

You can serve the Lord with your time

You can serve the Lord with your resources

You can serve the Lord with your energy

You can serve the Lord with your influence...

The list is endless. I think it's Apostle Joshua Selman who points out that if it was not for Joseph of Arimathea, the wealthy Jewish man who was a secret disciple of Christ—who used his influence to secure a tomb for Jesus—the Scripture about the resurrection of the Messiah would not have been fulfilled. God's interest would not have been established and advanced. For Jesus to rise on the third day, He needed to be buried first, and none of His known disciples had access to the level of influence that Joseph of Arimathea had. I would like to believe that wealth comes with influence! Most of us are familiar with Economics 101 from high school. The fact that there was a new tomb in which no one had been laid speaks to the law of supply and demand, and how that affected its accessibility and exclusivity. Let's look at the Burial of Jesus in John 19:38-42

> *Later, Joseph of Arimathea asked Pilate for the body of Jesus. Now Joseph was a disciple of Jesus, but secretly because he feared the Jewish leaders. With Pilate's permission, he came and took the body away. He was accompanied by Nicodemus, the man who earlier had visited Jesus at night. Nicodemus brought a mixture of myrrh and aloes, about seventy-five pounds.Taking Jesus' body, the two of them wrapped it, with the spices, in strips of linen. This was in accordance with Jewish burial customs. At the place where Jesus was crucified, there was a garden, and in the garden a new tomb, in which no one had ever been laid. Because it was the Jewish day of Preparation and since the tomb was nearby, they laid Jesus there.*

Like Joseph of Arimathea, you can serve the Lord where you are, with what you have. Isn't what being part of the body of Christ is after all? If you're still confused after such a powerful analogy then you might need to do some soul searching, and ignore the religious folks that still believe you only need to serve in the house of the Dear Lord.

While I am cognisant that this does not apply to all churches around the world, one of the reasons I stopped belonging to a church as an adult was fear, for myself.

I was afraid to lose myself.

I was afraid to gain acceptance and validation at church for being a good girl while I lost my essence in the process—my uniqueness,

my curiosity,

my thinking,

my courageousness,

my independence.

I was always the type that chose to stand for the truth even if it meant standing alone. As a result, I was called rebellious for standing my ground and refusing to conform in church as an adult… the cheeky child again. I was never afraid to create my path—a path that made me seek Jesus while He may be found, and call on Him on my own, while He is near. I carved a path for my children and their children's children—a path that still makes me talk to Him like a friend, and get to understand the mysteries of God that can only be found in the secret place of the Most High. Let's break down what church should be all about and call out the church bullies that resort to labelling people when they courageously choose relationship over religion.

Relationship with God = Spirituality.

Religion = Bondage.

Like this lady pastor that singled me out from a crowd one Sunday (still out to get me, Sunday, in my adulthood.) She said the Holy Spirit told her I needed Jesus—why? Perhaps she will tell us. My image and aura fitted her idea of a "sinner" and my outfit didn't exactly help. I mean, a woman dressed for church shouldn't be glamorous, right? No matter, what message are we relaying about this Jesus, other than the message of the cross? Here's the thing, idolatry is what God detests. "Thou shalt have no other gods before me." God is not against you having nice things—provided that nice things do not have you.

Glitz! Glam! Glory! Why is it hard to normalize? Is He meant to be only for the destitute? I thought He died for us ALL? The dangers of not thinking for yourself can lead to such ignorant assumptions:

Dress in rags—surely a child of God and therefore have all you need.

Dress in glam—poor thing has money but needs Jesus.

The day the church stops majoring in minors and starts looking to the crux of it all—the Gospel of Christ, and a personal relationship with God—perhaps I'd see myself going back to church on a full-time basis. For now, I still maintain, the solution is to dwell in the shelter of the Most High and rest in the shadow of the Almighty, instead of being present in church for roll call while you don't even know who you are in Christ.

IV

Part Four

Breaking off generational patterns

15

Necessary evil

Can we talk about school a bit? The importance of quality education. Choice of schools. As far as I understand, as a parent, you do your best to set your child up for success. When choosing a school, you consider the curriculum, the passing rate, the medium of instruction, the teacher-learner ratio just to name a few. Somehow I was still gullible enough to think given my wit, Elizabeth would send me where they would polish the black diamond in me. In contrast, I ended up in a school where hardly anyone passed and those that did were among my group, my study circle. If I say I was top of my class every year, top of my school, I must bear in mind it was not the best school but the crappy school I was put into by my parents. Tarkastad was and still is, no place for dreams or progress. To consider a career started early, at nursery school stage, had not caught on yet. This meant that even the most educated and liberated did not see the need to send their children to the only private school there was for their early education—Tarkastad High School. To make up for that, I suppose, or to try to catch up after higher primary (Grade 7 these days), they would send them to Tarka High. Up to that point—and continuing regardless—was the alternative.

Raymond Mhlaba.

Raymond Mhlaba was a public school, a disadvantaged one, with no resources, no hope for a bright future. It was more of a daycare for grown-up kids to keep them away from trouble during the day. At any given point in time, we had 50 students in a class, with one class teacher. We were taught every subject in our native tongue, IsiXhosa, but paradoxically, the final exam was always in English. Imagine being taught algebra and trigonometry in any African language! We would apply ourselves with the same due diligence to Shakespeare as we did to u*Thembisa noMakhaya*—English notwithstanding. To be or not to be, well... English was the question. "George" is the slang for English in my culture. No doubt it had something to do with King George. The chronic failure at Raymond to translate the curriculum to English was not only a comprehension problem on our part but "George" being as much of a challenge for our teachers also. It was like they needed to go to school before they could teach—since they too had never been taught English. Having known all this, my primary school teachers pleaded with Elizabeth not to send me to Raymond Mhlaba as they saw my potential—potential that could easily be wasted on such an abnormal public school. She pretended to see their point but cited "unaffordability" as her reason. And yet the mothers of some children who were domestic workers afforded the fees just fine—there was a payment plan made available for such cases. We need not concern ourselves with what my so-called father wanted for me but it says more than enough about my mother that my failure in life was more important to her than her success.

At all costs I was not to succeed, otherwise, she had failed. I was to be punished with Raymond Mhlaba. And here I was thinking books were my way out of here. And books would deliver me from my hell. In a school like mine, detention, merits and de-merits and prefects were foreign concepts.

We only had a class rep whose sole duty was to write a list of *Abangxolayo* (noise makers) in the absence of the teacher in charge—upon whose return a rod would not be spared. Yes! A rod was the substitute for both detention and de-merits! I soon got *gatvol* (fed up) of getting unwarranted beatings at school over and above the beatings I was getting at home. I was only 11 years old when I started Std 6 (Grade 8 now) in January, turning 12 in August 2001.

I've said it before and I say it again, I was officially what you would call a solemnly damaged child. I can't pinpoint or recall my first fight with one of the male teachers, I just know that I did not accept the rod where I felt it was unwarranted. Of course, no teacher would let you off the hook without a physical wrestling match. Oddly enough, I didn't mind getting beatings from female teachers—perhaps because they felt more like tickles than beatings. With their male counterparts on the other hand I was hell-bent on fighting them and gladly accepted the title of a hooligan when it came. I wasn't moved by any name-calling or unnecessary labels, I knew who I was. My monster of a step-father had not been able to beat that out of me.

Then there is the matter of mischief again and what I could and couldn't do if I set my mind to it. Perhaps I was born to it, I don't know, it played a part always in those times when I needed a push in the right direction. Or, I simply took whatever opportunities were being presented to me.

For example, we discovered a certain examination paper during evening classes, Maths Literacy, for the next day. Maths Literacy may sound like Maths but it was nothing like Maths. With Maths it was numbers and common sense and memorising formulae—laws of this and that and a bit of jargon—no comprehension of English required. I easily scored 90% on any given day. With Maths Literacy, on the other hand, I never scored more than 55% for any tests or assignments. And if that was what I was scoring, well… imagine the rest of the class. The paper was an early Christmas gift to us. We took it to the bush in the middle of the school yard—away from the classrooms and hundreds of eyes around us. To make sure no one followed us we put the word out that we wanted a safe quiet place to pray. If God could be used that way in church, I said, why not in school?

Prayer was the perfect masquerade to repel both attention and suspicion. We took turns to be watchmen from all four directions of the wind while each one carefully analyzed the sections that would be easier to memorize.

More than half the answers we had to Google and use a dictionary to try to make sense of the English that was used there. It took us almost the whole night to try and figure out the meaning of those answers so we could paraphrase. And of course, I had to warn them as the ringleader not to draw suspicion on themselves the following day. No one was to get more than 60% and those that were used to 30% should aim rather for 45%. It was a hard pill to swallow for my syndicate who were seeing 100% for the first time in their life.

During the exam, I had to continuously calm down my partners in crime as their hands were shaking and they were looking suspicious as the Maths Literacy teacher was storming in and out of the exam room looking livid. They were convinced we were busted and were ready to confess all. I was the only one to see his rage and restlessness had more to do with the bottle. He was way over tipsy but not drunk yet. In my time, in my school, it was normal for teachers to have brandy instead of tea at breakfast. Taking the opportunity again I was ready with my answer if we were caught: "Meneer, since you admire our dedication so much, you gave us the memo last night and asked us to promise not to tell." Bottom line, only four of us passed the Maths Literacy exam that day—and that was the only way.

The subject got phased out the following year due to the ridiculously low pass rate and we were happy to go back to Maths. My worst and best memory of high school was during my Matric year—worst in the sense that the last thing you expect when your school headmaster calls you into his office and locks the door behind you is for him to take out an *oukapie* (Okapi, a local brand of pocket knife made popular by gangsters) for you. It was to do with him doing his usual rounds through the classrooms like in the army when one of the teachers let slip how the money we paid for English textbooks (R500) was never used for the school.

Our headmaster was providing us instead with photocopies of the books—on the school's account—while pocketing the R500s. It's a no brainer, right? Our R500s should be refunded! It may sound like nothing now but R500 back then for a majority of unemployed parents was a lot of money, especially when our school fees were only R40 per month.

Yes, you counted right, R480 would cover a year's worth of school fees at Raymond Mhlaba. No doubt this was what my mother was thinking was affordable. As book smart as I was, I've always chosen street smart at any given time. I strongly believe you can only go so far with your books without a dose of street cred. Being street smart meant sitting with older boys who were all more than 4 years older than I was. I would keep them company sometimes when they smoked their weed during break time, which was a normal routine while covering their tracks when they screwed up.

We had pledged an unofficial allegiance: during or after school I had my bros look out for me. So one of them shouted from behind a desk: "We want our money back!" Then before you knew it the whole class started chanting and banging the desks: "We want our money! We want our money!" Oukapie's conscience must have told him what money we were alluding to because he turned red immediately and wanted to know who started all this. I'm not sure why he picked on me, unless because I was tiny and he thought he could bully me and I would presumably crack easily under interrogation? Without asking a question even he summoned me right there and then to his office—his biggest mistake.

Now, rewinding a couple of weeks before that, it must have been the end of the third term. He had singled me out of a crowd for wearing white socks with our green and gold uniform. He didn't bother coming to ask my reasons privately but was happy to mock me from the pulpit during what was their version of "final assembly". Every who's who from our township was there and I vowed to make him pay, and pay handsomely.

This was D-day, I was ready for him, only he had no idea. I will not lie and say I knew how to make him pay, I hadn't thought that far yet. But because I was ready for war, my strategy didn't matter. I was going for the jugular. I promised Boyce I wasn't about to sell him out—he must have been close to 23 years at the time when I was 16. He was doing a great job protecting me in the hood, not by his presence but our known affiliation. I did order a couple of "hits" that were necessary which he gladly executed in exchange for doing homework and assignments for him. Where I come, you hunt, or be hunted. I was a hunter. An undercover hunter.

Back to my headmaster's office, he kept spinning his *oukapie* in an attempt to scare me, and force a confession out of me. "You will have to tell me who told you about the R500's if you know what's good for you" he said, swinging his executive office chair at the same time. "I don't scare easily," I replied. Apparently I did not because he spilled now his guts in an effort to impress me with how dangerous he was, how notorious a gangster he was after hours. "Welcome to the club then" I responded.

By now he couldn't control his rage and that showed me he indeed had something to hide. He reminded me just so much of the caged animal that was my step-father working up steam for an attack. He was literally boiling, spilling over at the eyes and mouth, wiping his glasses, wiping saliva from his face—a weird, gross kind of involuntary salivation he's always had. I stood there calmly, calculating my next move. Not to engage in a vain dialogue but to show him who was the real gangster. And as if that decided him he abandoned the gangster route and came rather with his rod.

Strike one.

I was ready for what was to come. He was not the first male teacher to wrestle with. His aim was to cane me like any boy, citing "my balls" were bigger than his. My intention was not to fight back, there was no fun in that, I wanted to frustrate the hell out of him, and that's what I did.

Man to man, gangster to gangster, we locked horns. He was not much bigger than me but only stouter and seasoned over the years to bullying. There was no way he was going to wrestle me down and no way he was going to take a cane to me. There is a kind of passive resistance that in the face of violence and physical threats stands calmly contemptuous, unmoved by a mountain of bullies. A breed of fearless born of recklessness that doesn't care for the outcome but to stand your ground. I think that may have more to do with what I had learned along the way than what I had wanted to learn. Either way, it was good enough for me and more than a match for him. We wrestled like that, face to face, foe to foe, for some time. Maybe he saw like my step-father would, that thing in me that was fearless, and fearful too. And somehow, on a level only bullies operate from, he was afraid. And as if he recognised that, what I have just said, and how I have said it, he stepped back, walked straight to the door, unlocked it and opened it for me.

"Voetsek" (get out of my face) he said as he pointed me out.

Yes, I was thinking.

Strike two.

I was telling you about mischief and the kind of payment you need to make to yourself for wrongs suffered. How one who has suffered abuse over the years develops talents for revenge, creative outlets for reaping a vengeful harvest. Now that I had him where I wanted him I was ready to enjoy myself a little at his expense. I went back to class to my comrades, told them everything and gave instructions for what was to follow next: complete chaos! Why did I go to such lengths to turn the school upside down? I wanted to gauge just how powerful I could be. I could have easily found a way to make my headmaster pay for his sin but then what's vengeance without a little bit of fun? Perhaps you'll take me for a gangster, perhaps a criminal, perhaps a hooligan, perhaps a terrorist, I don't know, it's all good where I come from. It began as a *toy-toyi* song that turned into a war cry or even a cry for freedom or for justice, nothing else, nothing less. Frustrated as we were, hamstrung for all these years, what human being among us would not be with us? And it was amazing to see how in so short a time we had lit that fuse and the bomb was about to go off. How good it was to feel like we were vocal entities, people with power, with a voice! And suddenly the rod was in the other hand, the boot on the other foot. And now they were afraid and we were the : the ones calling the shots. It was pandemonium, but a healthy pandemonium, if you must choose. No desk was spared, no classroom, no teacher. Any voice daring to question us or ask if we were crazy was quickly silenced. No doubt in the apartheid days they would have identified me as an instigator and eliminated me before I even got started. But the fact of the matter is within a few minutes we had shut the entire school down—a school of more than 700 pupils. Then we took it to the streets and my crew had me on their shoulders, throwing me up in the air and catching me. I felt power I had never felt before. I felt invincible. I felt like a true gangster. Then in the middle of it one of our teachers called me aside and advised me to get a permit and report the protest to the police, else we'd go to jail. I gave him a big hug and off we went, leaving the rest of the school chanting. By the time the principal got to the police station to shut us down we had been granted our permission to protest. It was a legal strike! Again, he was outwitted.

Strike three.

Meanwhile, the police station had dispatched Sergeant Somana to defuse the strike. And here's where it gets hilarious because he was also one of the Elders at our church. Between home and church and school, well, what can I tell you? God was all over the place. He didn't get much time on the loudspeaker. He was talking about peace while we were talking about justice. Then he gave up on peace and went straight into preaching and that's when I raised my hand. Since I was somebody now and considered the instigator they gave me a platform to talk. I asked him if he was there as a member of Assemblies of God or South African Police Service. He's never spoken to me again till this day, and that's what…more than a decade ago? No doubt I was the instigator, I confess, take me out now while you can. I remember kindly demanding him to leave the school premises if he's not here to do what he's paid for. I had the entire school assembly behind me by now, chanting and supporting my order. I escorted him to the gate with a riot song, the school following after me. It made me think what the school is, or the church for that matter, or the town, if not the people. Elizabeth to the rescue. Elizabeth who in her wisdom had put me in here in the first place. Elizabeth who could not afford to put me anywhere else. Elizabeth who was concerned lest she spend any money on my future. Elizabeth whose clinic was barely a two minute walk from the school. Elizabeth who they thought would diffuse my passion. Only to fuel it. Talk about revenge. A dish you eat cold. The look on her face? Worth a thousand beatings. Worth a thousand times when she had turned her face away and pretended I did not exist. Or wished I had never existed to begin with. But here I was. In her face. Fully, fully, magnificently, in her face. At the tender age of what? 16? Steve Biko, where are you now? Where are you now. Black consciousness? She wanted the floors to open up so they could swallow her. But what? No hymn? No *"Lord my God? When I in awesome wonder...?"* Like when our eyes met under the train, when the window opened on her reality, and I saw what was in her, who she was. She was convinced I was demonically possessed. As if she hadn't seen the so-called demonically possessed in church. As if I hadn't seen it at home in my own house. That I must no doubt still go back to. But not right now, no. Not today. Not while I sit on top and look down on you. And I have the whole world at my command. I didn't leave it there. Press in, as they say, for the kill. I went as far as calling the department of Education to report Oukappie for the maladministration of funds. I had all the proof I needed to get the department's attention. You'll know by now a 16-year-old me was resourceful enough to acquire that evidence. Fast forward a year later, fired and allegedly charged over multiple fraud and embezzlement charges not only for our school but for the previous schools he'd been chowing money from.

Strike 4?

What I did came at a cost, a cost I wasn't ready for, a cost that is still following me till this day, only it has no bearing on me. All my high school teachers—except for one—supported him and hated me for taking him on. Were they also in on it? I don't know. You can't embezzle on that scale without others being involved. Of course, some where just plain gullible and took him for a saint since he had a high rank in his church, it was said. What they didn't know was, I could see a two-faced hypocrite from a mile away. And isn't it funny once again that you can have a gangster and a headmaster and a church man all in the same breath, as if they belonged together? Not funny where I come from, but the norm. The one thing I had going for me was they couldn't fail me. Top of my class, top of my school, doesn't fail.

But they could do their best to keep me out of university. And that they did with every evil intent they could muster, colluding together to fabricate my results so that a year of A grades became suddenly C grade for my Matric. I went suddenly from being a straight A student to a C student throughout, denying me four years of prevailing against impossible odds. My one way out of hell was here, in my books, but they would deny me that too. Because I dared not be relegated to that place where they were in their minds—a place they have not escaped from today. They eliminated us one by one. Every one who had taken part in the riot, the ring leaders. One by one they left until it was just me, alone. And I wonder if up to now that is not what I am and not what I was intended to be. I bled, but that didn't break me. I bled but it didn't bleed me. Hated in my home town, hated by the majority who took Oukappie for a saint—denying my claims till the very end—it didn't silence me. I was not about to be caged and silenced by cowards and a misinformed group of people who had no right to fiddle with my destiny like that. Thinking back, I think what it was I did for them and what it was they had to punish me for. I think of the good I may have done for others and the good I did for them. I think of an enemy of us all that unfortunately uses us to do his dirty work. I think of the few of us who stand alone and who are labelled criminals and rebels. I think then of Jesus and I think yes, I'm on the right track. Always have been. From the beginning.

16

The snare was broken

Back to reality. Back to the future. I had gone as far as contemplating suicide before. Elizabeth had all sorts of powerful medication she brought home from work. I was asking myself serious questions, questions no teenager should have to ask. Did I really want to take my own life and stop living? Or did I want to end the version of life that I was living? That sounds mature for a teen but the life I had lived up to then had propelled me ahead of my time. As soon as I realised I didn't want me to die, but that version of me that was exposed to misery and suffering, I could make a decision. Isn't that the case with suicide?

To wish miraculously that your current self would die and give birth to a new self, a new life altogether?

And I wonder in that sense if that is not what Christ was talking about when he was talking about being born again. Death to self and a beginning of new life. My suffering was the result of a bully step-father, it was simple math to any dummy—kill the bully, end your suffering. He was not worth dying for, that's what I kept on telling myself. I was not about to let him win. He had been trying to kill me throughout my hellish upbringing, he just never had the guts to go for a straight kill—typical coward. I started believing somehow that the fearlessness he pretended not to see in me must have scared him. He was scared of me, I kept telling myself until I believed it. By the age of 16, I had passed my Matric and kept the promise I made to myself.

Tarkastad you could say was the middle of nowhere. Also the middle of the universe. The universe sent me to Cape Town. Cape Town could just as easily have been a distant constellation and from there my home town was as far removed from me as a black hole. It's just as well because it was the beginning of my independence and emancipation. Tarkastad had what? Lots of dust and mountains. Lots of thorn trees and rocks. Stony ground, dry desert ground, desert skies. Not that one would ever look up much—life was too close to the ground. No doubt there was a mountain and it meant something to me—a mountain looking on like an old fossil. Here there was a mountain too and another thing… a sea. Two oceans met there at the tip of the continent and I wonder if here two worlds would meet for me too, two mighty undercurrents, and here one would be able to choose between one and the other. And find one's self again. It's a small world they say, I don't know about that. It's a small universe. Out of all the stars out there, out of all the constellations, I made two friends who came from where I was coming from. Not that anyone ever could come from where I was coming from, but the same region we call the Eastern Cape, my province. They were two and three years older than I was respectively and on another level academically but we were soon three musketeers.

Knowing my high school background you know I came into university life from the background of being worth nothing academically and bound to fail any university course I took, let alone law and psychology, which happened to be what I was good at. And I knew that from where I was, looking out at that distant constellation leading me ever on toward my destiny. You'll know also my parents and teachers—society at large—had done everything they could to make it impossible for me to be here in the first place. Hell hath no fury as Raymond Mhlaba scorned. On top of my struggles at home, my struggles at school had been downgraded, invalidated.

On top of being the Raymond Mhlaba girl, I was the average Raymond Mhlaba girl. My fabricated marks told me there was no hope for me. And I would stay in my clay pit forever. So my friends, while coming from the same region, came from different worlds. Their private school education created those worlds but I saw the power of my imagination bridging them again—one for all, all for one. We'd sit on the grass after class and discuss what we had heard during the day but their language was all Greek to me. The language was the barrier more than anything else. They spoke the language of the city while I was just a grassroots girl. I soon realized what we called English where I came from was actually Minglish.

You get broken English—easily excused—then Minglish. Minglish takes one look at you and breaks you down and puts you back and breaks you down and puts you back again indefinitely, no matter how kind you try to be.

There's no understanding Minglish, nor Minglish understanding you.

Whether it was the confidence of being under the illusion of speaking English or the humour of the language itself, I don't know. There I was, having to adjust not only to university life but to city life. Between the bright lights and the flashy cars, I can't tell you which one made me feel more out of place. How I got here, how I escaped from where I was, how I extricated myself from one environment and got myself into another, God knows.

I was still speaking to Elizabeth however, my one and only connection to where I was coming from. No matter what history, what life experience, still, Elizabeth was Mama. Mama was Elizabeth. And I was far from home. I called her one day in excitement. I had needs of course but also I wanted to hear her voice and share with her my new life. The excitement ended when I mentioned money.

"Mama, I need R50 for a course reader," I said.

"Yoh! So much money?" she replied.

I still can't say who was more disappointed that day or who was supposed to be. Maybe with a change of scene and a change of worlds I had thought she would step in with a new start. Eternally hopeful, eternally optimistic, eternally pathetic, believing forever for the best and never preparing for the worst. I think that's the saddest thing about children. Believing for the best and never stopping believing but never ever seeing a reason to believe. I think the greatest gift a child has from his parents is faith and when they take it away from them they take everything. There's only one thing a parent can ever give his or her child and that is reason to believe. It said something that at this point that I still believed and had not yet given up hope. I kept at it for a while in the hope it would change but the illusion was finally shattered. It called for a meeting again between Me, Myself and I and we decided to stop nagging her and face the reality that I was somehow running away from: if Elizabeth wouldn't buy me a school bag as a child living under her roof, what made me think she would buy me a course reader? Shoes are an important thing in a girl's life and I wonder how far she went in my childhood to make me feel that I was not that girl but something not worth anything at all—something deserving of nothing at all—that must walk barefoot on the ground?

In high school I had avoided making a spectacle of myself by taking my classmates' hammy-down shoes year in and year out until they gave in. It was that or show up with shoes that looked like hungry baby crocodiles—no offence to reptile lovers. Oddly enough, I never felt humiliated or embarrassed. Humiliation it is said remains a common form of punishment, abuse and oppression. I have my own hypothesis: like rejection, humiliation is a choice. No one can reduce you to feel small and have all these unpleasant feelings about yourself without your permission. My question for you is, why voluntarily subject yourself to punishment, abuse, and oppression? When you can choose sympathy, compassion, and liberty? It's all in my head, I reckoned. All in my imagination. In my head I was convinced I was wearing the most expensive leather shoes—prickly thorns along the way forever fishing for new angles to enter my skin a minor distraction. I believed it and that fuelled my self-esteem and self-confidence as a child—I had nowhere else to look for it. A positive mindset is everything, I can attest to that. You may be unable to control your negative thoughts but you have all the power in the universe to control the thoughts you hold onto. I chose to hold onto my positive thoughts—my fuel at university. On my own financially, I looked for part-time jobs to finance my way. My grades had earned me a place in university but my parents were not forthcoming—at least so far as money was concerned. For them to take the credit and the glory—and whatever else came with my success—was to be expected but meanwhile there was printing and photocopying expenses and things like where to stay and how to stay and how to eat and how to move—how to stay alive basically. My plan was to find assistance through bursary programs or any kind of student support scheme that came my way. Elizabeth had managed the registration fees but that was it. From here on I was on my own— sweet sixteen and *"empty as a pocket, empty as a pocket and nothing to lose."* I had been staying up to this point with her family in Cape Town, another long story I am sure one day I will tell you about. I squatted there for the first nine months until it became unbearable. "I don't have to stand for this crap" I said to myself one morning and packed my bag and moved across to one of my musketeers. I never said goodbye and I never saw them again. It's been 16 years now. At 16 I was an "over-achiever" and "under-age" according to the labour laws. I'm wondering now what it means to be an overachiever if not someone who just wanted to get the hell away from home as soon as she could. I had taken books for my way out and here I am writing again. As for underage what age was it you needed to be not to drive wheelbarrows? Having driven myself like my devil step-father, having catapulted myself out from my predicament, I now needed to do like they do in the army—hurry up and wait.

I suppose you could say this was a blessing turned into a curse but I will say there was a blessing still in it, since I learned a costly life lesson: be careful what you ask for. Are you ready to carry the burden that comes with your blessing? Rest assured, you don't get the one without the other. Talk about laws, the unwritten law for me was: no one bothered to tell me about life. I had to find out as it happened what to do next. With no study guides or photocopies of textbooks my study options were limited. Exams were not waiting either.

Knowing I had nothing to fall back on propelled me to think of solutions rather than regurgitating the problem over and over. I called for a family meeting in my head and concluded: *girlfriend, the aim is to pass, not to prove a point.* From there, I knew what I had to do. I used our lunch-hour to skim through my fellow musketeers' textbooks as we ate and fooled around as freshmen. The focus would be the material that was likely to show up on the exam paper and the sections that wouldn't require Noah's genealogy "...the son of ... the son of..." etc. In plain English I gambled on the odds being in my favour. After all, isn't that how the portfolio fund managers on the stock market outperform their benchmarks? If they can be trusted in their field of expertise, could I not too? It's not as if I had no track record of my own. Like a fund manager I would juggle one set of risk and return variables against the other and place my bets. Like a fund manager I encountered volatility—a rough, cruel lesson to learn at my age. And in this case no luxury of holding asset allocation meetings and portfolio review forums. I was no quant analyst to be running risk analysis reports either.

Consistency had to be my currency. It was no longer about being the smartest in the lecture room but the most inventive. It was about my survival! My strategy succeeded for the first semester but going into the second I quickly had to change tack. My musketeers during this time were all I had, my life support in many ways, but I've told you about temporary relief. Like those gloves during the brick burning process were the books of these, my fellows. But I knew always at some point the books were going to be taken back and made unavailable. And really, without the books, what was I doing there? The fact of the matter is without those books I was nothing—my hopes at least were dashed. And everything depended on my hopes. You may say where were my parents, where was my family, you know the answer, there weren't any. It was just me and my books and now my books were taken away from me. I was a village girl again. A township girl. No spoiled brat. My friends couldn't see me as ever being anything more than that. They allowed me their books because they felt sorry for me, poor disadvantaged urchin. But really I was only surviving. Then the results came back, time after time, top of the pack again. What was it with this township girl? You can't blame them at lunchtime saying "no, we need our books too, find your own." But it was really no different to any attempt of my so-called father to hold me back. I didn't blame them, there were no feelings of resentment. I was grateful for their generosity. Only I wasn't what they were and they could at least have given me credit for that. The withdrawn support now triggered all the old feelings of temporary relief. Emergency meeting in my head: *guys, what next?*

Answer: *Pivot!*

Our exams were three hours long and you would be disqualified to sit for your exams if you were an hour or more late. This left me with 50 minutes for studying a 700-page textbook, 5 minutes for meditation and prayer and pulling myself together and 60 seconds for sprinting to the exam room. We'd normally leave our school bags outside with our books and go in but here I was last in the queue to snatch the books I needed from my musketeers. I could have asked them of course but for what? One for all and all for one no longer applied. It was now each one for himself, do or die. Rush to the bathroom. Open a cubicle. Sit on the seat. Open the books. Read through the notes. Absorb, absorb, absorb. Process and disseminate. Maintain peace of mind. Maintain self-control. These were the staples of my life, my jet fuel and jet plane. In that hour I was not only a student but a life coach, a motivational speaker and a cheer-leader—from me, by me, to me, for me—my new normal for the rest of my second semester. But what prayer was I praying? And to who? This was no prayer of desperation is one thing—I'd been desperate before and certainly knew what it looked like. I couldn't afford to be desperate because from that place I couldn't possibly be productive. I've always found desperation a counterproductive exercise. This was a prayer of impossibility! I knew it was impossible to absorb all the overload of information in such a short space of time and rely on my working memory. And not just any information but mostly new information. PowerPoint lectures provided only summaries of textbooks with no glossaries. I now had to study the concepts and the jargon buried into the concepts. And there were formulae I needed to memorize. It was all too much for one mind to process. I knew from my study group in high school it was practically impossible to register information from the first round of studying. Short-term memory is not equipped for that—it can only store memory for 20 to 30 seconds. My working memory, on the other hand, was overly active at this time. I would be studying multiple chapters at once—using my fingers as book markers—flipping back and forth through the textbook. This was humanly impossible but I had to tap into the little girl that was once caged as an animal and worked like a slave—who believed that you could bend anything you want to your will if you're hungry enough. I must bend the laws to my will, the universe also, but for that I needed the universal forces to be on my side.

I needed God to intervene and approve. I wasn't concerned much about the details, there was no luxury of time to be concerned anyway—even if I wanted to. The details of how He was going to do it didn't matter.

Whether He was going to make time stand still from the moment I walked out that toilet door and took a seat in the exam room or if He would extend the 20-30 seconds window to 55 minutes, I didn't know.

My only job was to believe it was all possible. And that was my prayer, if any! If God could ride on the clouds and Peter defy the laws of the gravity, surely I could.

What's interesting though, I wasn't praying to God as my Lord—this was the time I hated Him! I was praying to Him as part of my "where were you when I needed you as a little girl?"

It was a "you owe me big time for being so cruel to me, you better prove that you're not as cruel as I know you to be." After all, as much as I had been convinced at this stage that God was cruel, I never doubted that He was all powerful, that both might and power are in His hands.

If I were to put one word to my freshman year I would say jungle. Only the laws of the jungle applied. But others emerged to encapsulate my strategy to survive.

"Wash daily from nose tip to tail tip. Drink deeply, but never too deep. Remember the night is for hunting and forget not the day is for sleep." Survival of the fittest they say. Eat or be eaten. Kill or be killed. I don't know. I had survived all that. Only the strongest survive? I dare to refute this. No doubt I was not the strongest but as for the fittest, well… I made the shortlist. But what kept me going and what got me to the finishing line was not being fit but being consistent.

There's a mathematical formula for consistency that puts to numbers what we cannot do with letters. I saw it a couple of years back on a Facebook post. Doing nothing at all versus making small consistent efforts:

(1.00) x 365 = 1.00 vs. (1.01) x 365 = 37.7

Do I need to say more? I think not! My small, consistent efforts paid off, all I had to do was to imagine the end: me progressing to the second academic year.

17

The land of milk and honey

ugust arrived, my birthday month, 17 years behind me, four months away from passing my first year. How had I survived? I hope this book will tell you. We tend to rush through the story and not go into details, we feel we don't have time for that, or we don't want to go back to that or they are not important. But you know, it's those details again. Those details go into telling your story. And into you too. Since you are your story. And what better birthday could it have been for me to find what I found at this watershed age of 17? Here's a thing, I've been focused, right?

My whole life had only been about surviving and how to survive and not looking for anyone, to anyone, for help. No Prince Charming or knight in shining armour. No saviour to the rescue. And in the telling of this story I have not tried to paint any other picture but the reality, in as few words as possible. But now, well… maybe you will indulge me. Maybe I will indulge myself. Just for a minute or two.

It all started with the big toe on my right foot. It had been swollen for some days and slowing me down in the mornings.

A big toe you can say. A right foot. A leg that was dragging. Not what I needed to get into class. Not what I needed in life. But as it says… "a man may make his plans but the Lord directs his paths."

So I missed the bus that day and rushed now to the taxi rank to try to catch it, dragging my leg along like a ball and chain. And isn't that really what I was dragging all along? And wasn't it dragging behind me now, preventing me from getting to my lectures? Preventing me from getting on with my life? And escaping the hell that still loomed for me if I failed? You understand the pressure that was always on me from the moment I arrived in Cape Town. *Fail here and you fail forever.* It's those little things—this way or that way—that change your life forever. Well, change my life forever it did.

Little did I know that on this day the heavens had orchestrated my delay in my favour. I caught the next bus and as we got to campus I met… OK, I'll save the cheerleading for later.

I suppose I must tell you at least a little bit about myself. I was focused and intent on only one thing—to escape the hell I was coming from. Love interests or romance itself was the least of my priorities. As for love, well… I wasn't exactly coming into any man's life with anything to offer. Only one hell of a story, literally. That nobody wanted to hear. So he appears in my life here like a shadow almost, another obstacle or hindrance in my way, blocking my way forward, distracting me from my goal.

I never saw anything in my life at this point as anything but an obstacle or a hurdle I needed to get over without tripping myself over it.

He approached me and tried to make small talk about my limping, offering to carry my school bag. I was not impressed. If anything, I got all feisty and irritated by the small talk—offended to think he was implying I could not take care of myself. Independence, after all, was one thing at least I could rely on.

He was not put off. If anything, the short treatment encouraged him. I persisted with one-word answers to send a clear "I'm not interested" message. Still, he took it lightly, for a joke.

Let him laugh at his jokes I thought to myself, he would get nothing from me. Turned out me trying to turn him off turned him on! Imagine! Like I was just playing hard to get. Meanwhile, I only wanted him out of my way and out of my life. You tell me how he got it right, I have no idea, they say God is the Ageless Romancer—well, maybe it was Him, I don't know. Certainly, he displayed patience and that to me was a sign of confidence, humility, and respect.

I eased up a little. Let thaw the freeze.

Let loose a smile for his encouragement. All teeth now, bright-eyed and bushy-tailed. *How easy* you may be thinking—as he may have been thinking—to get a girl to smile. But it was for his cockiness. *Plucky little rooster you, here's a feather for your cap.* I wonder today still about that smile. I mean, there were smiles in my life for this one and that one, smiles in conversation smile no doubt among musketeers, but that one for him, well... that may have been the beginning and end of it.

It didn't matter to him what kind of smile it was or for what or for who. A smile from the dragon was enough. Enough to lighten up his day he would have said. Like the sun shining. And for me not to be smiling was like the sun going down. Or passing behind a cloud. I'm not sure how it happened or why it happened so quickly but from that moment we became inseparable.

A person had come into my life as if he had always been there. Only he had not been there in the way he was now. Is that not true love? It was not love at first sight either, or a happy ever after fairy tale. He was nothing out of a concocted romance novel—my world was the opposite of that.

There was just something about him.

Something like solid rock. A rock I could rely on. There's that parable about a house built on rock, was this not it? The rock of love?

And how many storms would still come, and how many seas, to crash against that house? For the house still to stand? But here's the funny thing, I was not looking for a husband and neither was he looking for a wife. I've got this strong feeling that may be why we are together today.

It was never about marriage or getting married but about us and what we were to each other when we had no such idea of love in mind. There was no pressure on us or questions about what our future held as a couple. For the first time, I was able to live in the moment and enjoy it for what it was. And I don't know if there is any better gift or any better thing that could have happened to me at this time. Talk about a birthday month. After lectures, we'd sit and talk for hours through the afternoon. Imagine me just finding time to relax and sit and talk! Able for once to put studies aside! And just be human! I still can't stop thinking about it. That birthday present. Of him. Like a big strong castle made of stone and inside the walls you could talk and be free for as long as you like—nothing was going to get to you there. I don't know what other thing there is in heaven but here was heaven for me. And if I was like the sun to him was he not the universe to me? He would listen not only attentively but actively, without interrupting.

The day would go by so fast that we would go our separate ways close to midnight—just in time for him to catch the last bus home. I'm no Cinderella fan, you've noticed, I care nothing for fairy stories—my life has been too real—but here was Prince Charming needing to get home before midnight. There's something to be said for a man who only wanted to be with me to listen and to hear me out and take as much time as he could before getting the last ride home. There's something here about investment and seeing a return on your investment. This was no charming, no frog dressed up in a suit, but the original solid rock article. The more time we spent together, the closer we became. I opened up to him about my childhood and he listened empathetically, without judging. We were coming from two different worlds no doubt but somehow we had commonalities. From the first day, we started dating he'd buy me lunch every single day and verify if I had something reserved for dinner. And he didn't do it from a point of pity but a place of love.

It was easy for me to know the difference because by this time I could afford to buy myself a plate of food. Remember, food had been used as a weapon against me growing up. I had been made to feel like I did not belong like I did not deserve to eat. Not like a human being anyway. Like the dog would be fed they would feed me, but not the meat. Or like a pig with my face shoved into the pig food. Food, you can understand, was a thing in my life. If I could live without it I would, and mostly I have. "Food I have that you do not know of" said Christ. But here was a man not using food as a weapon but as an offering. It was reassuring for me to know that there was someone interested in me for who I was—concerned for my welfare. It's such a worn-out little word that welfare, it's hardly ever used for what it was intended. What kind of a welfare worker was it up to now that had been my mother? I have a problem today with adults being served before children. For me, it should be the other way around. When the children have food and are eating, the adults can afford to eat. But the priority was skewed in my house. Here the head of the house ate first and ate as much as he could before the children got to eat. Then the meat was all gone and it was just gravy and Elizabeth dishing up and making excuses.

This was my first time feeling and being seen. It was my first time to realize that I was special. He opened my world to so many possibilities.

But still, the happily-ever-after fairy tale of marriage and children were not on the cards. I hated marriage and the idea of having children and so did he—even though his reasons were different from mine. For the first time I was happy and my human need for a sense of belonging was fully met. I would listen to his love talk for days, to the poetry that bubbled from his heart, or we would simply sit in silence while our souls communicated in ways that are indescribable.

I can't tell you at what stage we fell in love or realized we were soul mates. But I remember the stomach butterflies and the weak knees and the way he looked at me when our eyes met and the smile he could not control. We would talk on the phone for hours, every day. I was amazed. Here I was finding a soul mate I didn't look for, experiencing the love I never knew existed, enjoying chemistry that was out of this world. Our bond only grew stronger with time and it soon became obvious we were in it for the long haul. Relationships on campus were less about commitment than conquest. I came, I saw, I conquered—veni, vidi, vici—move on to the next conquest. But here was a man who saw less conquest than a contest.

He could see a partner with her own mind and along the way the two minds would meet. I remember those days with affection. Here, at last, was a lover for my soul. I have no words to tell you exactly what that means but it goes deep. There was something about having this little room and a mattress and just about nothing else. There was yet a day when there was to be a duvet. This was my new home and here was my life. My shell of a house was nothing but me and what spirit I put into it.

But here a man had entered and here a man brought a one-handled pot. I had no pot at all and for me the pot was pot enough. It did the job of cooking whatever it was and it cooked it for as long as we could not replace it with a two-handled pot. And when we could I gladly passed it on to a fellow housemate. It may yet be doing a job of work for somebody on campus, that pot, and have a story also to tell. Soon we had other things and here we made a little home for ourselves. It really doesn't take much to be happy as a human being when love is with you and flowing and giving and receiving and trusting and believing for the best. As I say, marriage had never been my strong point. What resulted from marriage should never be subjected to marriage. Children should not suffer, I had said, the sins of the parents. If children could be born to the world any other way it would have been better, I said. Better not to be born at all, than to be the product of marriage.

But something had happened here.

My world-view had begun to shift. And maybe my view of the planet had changed, and the inhabitants of the planet. Perhaps there was some reason to it all after all.

Fast forward, we experienced a sudden change of heart about marriage and children. It was like our hearts had taken over and left our reasoning out of it. By the time I was ready to consider marriage I was very aware of what I was signing up for. I had seen my husband's dark side and was at ease about it. He had seen mine too and could handle it. We spent six years together before committing ourselves. Timelines didn't matter to us as long as we had each other. What we found intriguing—and what gave marriage this awful stigma—was two people with two different sets of values, belief systems, views of the world, suddenly put under one roof and expected to make it work overnight. If not, they get divorced. We can talk about farming and preparing the ground for planting here. Preparation time is essential for any relationship to take root. The seed of love must find the soil and grow out of soil that is well nurtured, well-tended, and watered. Preparing the ground for marriage enables the plant to grow and bear fruit in season. But mostly we rush in and what we get out of it has no root at all but is quickly uprooted and blown away.

Can we not just give it time and do whatever spadework is necessary before we commit to planting? In our case it was six years of fighting rough battles. The option of breaking up if you couldn't take it any more was freely available. We pushed past the honeymoon phase toward a mature relationship with ups and downs that we managed like surfers floating up and down on an ocean swell.

We moved from whose belief systems would now rule us to whose values made more sense. I was hell-bent on insisting no man will ever tell me how to live my life and my husband, being a traditional man, had no intention of taking instructions from a woman. Who would win?

Who would get their way?

Who would end up the winner and the other the loser? How many relationships have never got past this stage? It's natural for one to feel that they must stand their ground and hadn't I done so already, and wasn't it necessary? But with marriage, there is no ground of your own but the ground of both of you. You stand for the marriage, not for yourself. Or there is no marriage. So for some time we battled along, neither of us willing to relinquish what they thought was right. There is the need to be right that is wrong and the willingness to be wrong that is right. We realized at last that marriage is not about being right at all but about being respectful, respecting our common ground.

Also, we realized that marriage is not a status symbol but a symbol of commitment. Culturally one may be looked down on or frowned upon if you are not married and do not have a husband or wife. But it is better to be alone than to be in a relationship for the wrong reasons— to make commitment your goal as opposed to being seen to be together when in fact you are not. Pushing on, forever moving forward, never standing still, we learned our lessons. We were growing toward a union, a perfect union, that would survive any storm. I've seen people getting married all around me expecting in no time at all to magically become "one" as per the *two shall become one*. There is no magic to this, it takes faith, renewal of the mind, selflessness, hard work, concerted efforts, determination, and commitment. With our foundation laid we were happy to enter into the contract of marriage without the baggage of external pressures and lame timelines that would be meaningless and irrelevant in the end. Marriage is not an accomplishment but a blessing. And you don't look for it, it finds you. The consciousness of this informed our decision to get married and subsequently start a family. Looking at our four beautiful children, how could we have imagined having them 17 years ago?

Pushing on, pressing on, still higher, still further, forever growing, forever moving forward, the one who showed me how to love myself showed me also how to love our children.

To navigate the stormy straits of motherhood with no point of reference required a steady hand at the wheel. Together we pushed on, pushed through—one of the hardest things I ever had to do. It's hard enough that no one can prepare you for motherhood or supply you with an instruction manual. It's harder still with different personalities requiring different approaches. It's hardest having no example at all to draw from, no pattern to follow. Unless it was the pattern I fell into growing up. And really, that was the last thing I wanted for my children.

It was only later on in motherhood, that I discovered I actually learnt everything I needed to know about being a mother from Elizabeth, just in reverse.

I say that because there were times when I would unconsciously fall into her bad habits but with my husband to guide me and to point out the difference I soon became conscious, quick to get myself back in order. Being abused as a child and a young adult was no excuse for me to take it out on innocent children.

I knew I needed to face my monsters before perpetuating the cycle of a loveless motherhood. So to all woman-beaters out there, I have something to say: being abused as a child or growing up watching your father beating the hell out of your mother does not qualify or give you the licence to do the same to your spouse. That goes for wounded mothers too: you know the pain of being raised from a place of brokenness and unresolved generational traumas instead of love, why poison your children with more pain? You know better, do better!

133

18

Standing my ground

December 2006, end of my first year at university, at the age of 17. I was fortunate enough to avoid going back to my hell-home for the mid-term break, I can't exactly recall how I managed to pull that off, but now I had nowhere to hide, nowhere to run—I had to go back and play happy families. Not having seen my parents for almost 12 months was like an early Christmas gift for me. University had been a new world, a new life, challenging as ever, but a change from everything I knew. As good as a holiday for me and I never wanted it to end. I recall the anxiety of leaving my new life behind, my new normal while embracing the fear of what might go wrong where I was going. I dreaded losing the licence to my freedom and immersed myself rather in the wonderful memories of Cape Town, from making new friends to what I suspected was too good to be—Ree. The fact that we were coming from two different worlds was sufficient for me to conclude that it was all one big prank and was bound to be temporary. There was no way someone like him would want a damaged township girl like me that didn't bring much to the table except misery. I didn't have wonderful childhood stories to share with him as we sat under the stars in the evenings.

For Ree, it was hard to comprehend the dysfunctionalities of my family as someone that put a different meaning to family. To him, family had been everything. His aunts and uncles all treated him like a prince. I was never able to tell from a distance when he was speaking to his mother or his aunt. Love seemed to be at the source of it and with that a sense of well-being and security and being well provided for—cushioned from the harsh reality of my life that was so much in contrast to his and me so opposite. His smile, his face, the light in his eyes, teleported me to a world I was not ready for: unconditional love. How was I to get involved with someone that was so loved? Where would I begin offering him what I didn't have myself? He doubtlessly knew what love looked like and would certainly recognize what was far from love. These were my first impressions. Ree was the product of some good things that had happened in his life. If it was all good or if there was more to it that I was not seeing, he will tell. Like the one handled pot, he too has his story. Here he was, his heart was overflowing with light and love, mine with wrath and acrimony. The same way he was oozing with confidence I was pulling him down for the lack of it.

Logically, if I were to offer him what I had—all of me—it meant returning his love with the opposite of love. *He deserves better* I thought to myself as I sifted through all our beautifully captured memories on my old Nokia phone. I wanted time to stop turning and the sun to stand still in the sky as we approached Cradock. My 900km buffer between heaven and hell was now 90km. We were entering the conflict zone. No more stops between me and home! Cradock passed by, Tarkastad 70 km. My stomach churned within me at the thought of seeing the "Welcome" sign appear.

There was no time for reflection now, no space for memories, only preparing myself for battle. You will know if you have suffered trauma on the level I have for such a long time.

You will know what a lifetime of abuse can do for your nervous system. My body couldn't tell the difference between my thoughts and reality, I know that because I was no longer in control—I tried so hard to calm down and hope for the best but my body went ahead of me.

My knees started shaking, my heart pounded at a rate I had never experienced before, I began sweating while everyone else on the bus was cuddled in blankets against the chilly dawn of this small wilderness town. Then a lightning bolt through my seat, across my forehead, welcoming me back to the lightning zone. The phone in my lap was a lightning conductor, my body a conduit, every nerve ending an extension of the lightning fork. Ree checking in to find out if I had arrived safely!

To hear his voice, God knows, what was it like for Moses? In my heightened state of consciousness, my involuntary response was terror—it sounded like he was saying his goodbyes—like he knew he would never see me again. The call didn't last for more than 30 seconds but in that time I downloaded enough to take it to earth. I would never see him again, I knew. The way he said "I love you" was different, it carried so much emotion.

If I were to name it I'd say it was a "good luck, it was good while it lasted" kind of emotion. I had briefed him about my domestic abuse and child slavery, I had felt compelled to share some information about myself.

Unfortunately, I had nothing better to tell. I sobbed bitterly in the bus with no regard for the passengers as I entered my home town. I knew I was finished. The life I had in Cape Town was a fairy tale. I had to get back to reality. There is a reality here, a stark reality, and a sense of history. The beauty you have all around you and above you and the sky seems to say *I have been here for as long as the earth has.* And the mountains say *not so long.* Looking down on you like a grumpy old maid she seems to say *not yet. Still a little bit longer, my child. Secrets we all have that no one will ever know anything about.* At last, I stepped down from the bus like a man stepping onto the moon. "One small step for me, one great step for mankind."

I was inhaling anxiety and exhaling fear as I boarded a taxi from the bus stop. I was now home. There was no turning back. Welcome? Well yes, there was a welcome. Surprisingly warm it was, as the sun, but in winter. A cold sun with cold shadows. A sun with memories. And painful reminders. Things went quickly back to how I left them only now no child slavery. Like somehow they got intimidated by this person that I had suddenly become. That's exactly the thing with change! Sometimes all you need is a different environment to germinate your metamorphosis.

I had not realized I had changed in such a short space of time. What can I tell you about our monster? 12 months was a very short break when you'd been caged, tortured, and tormented perpetually for 16 years.

Hints were being dropped about how I should not be going back to Cape Town. They said it was premature and inappropriate for a minor to stay away from her parents. This was after my "very concerned" step-father had seen my academic transcript for the year. It was no secret he had secretly hoped I'd fail and come back deflated. With the passive approach not working for him, he fell back once more to bully pulpit tactics and forbade me from going.

Can you imagine? What did it have to do with him that I was there in the first place? And if I decided to stay there or not? Did he think I would forever be under him, subject to his whims? But I had found my voice. I had found something else also—the power to stand my ground.

Ask me what that power is? I will say, love. I raised my objection and in retaliation, the filthy puddle that was his thought life—the cesspit that was his self-loathing—spilt over again. He told me I had been whoring all year long and wanted to go back to my numerous sexual partners in Cape Town. Now that, no doubt, would have been what he would have done if he were me. Since he wasn't, I didn't bother explaining to him that with the amount of school work I had— playing catch up with life skills more developed than mine—there was no chance of miraculously turning into a whore even if I wanted to. How often would Ree help me with my assignments, typing for me while I kept him company? That was the closest we ever got to quality time. But then he wouldn't know that, would he? Quality time for him was time he spent with his long leather belt. It got worse. His sewer outlet knew no other outlet. Now I was back he was paranoid cop again, chief inspector, paranoid about me and sex in the same breath. Now I was forbidden to take a bath. He could only have said that for one reason: what he was going to say next. "Unless you're trying to wash away the smell of all your men off your body, you have no reason to wash." This made me realize if I opened the room and entertained this gibberish one more time, I'd be his prisoner for the rest of my life, just like Elizabeth.

It was now or never.

Here was my turning point. My standing ground.

I have to go back to Cape Town I told myself. Ree had been calling but we barely had time to talk. I was being watched like a hawk. Or maybe a whore? Who knows? My tuition fees for the year had not been covered and I brought that up. Elizabeth had paid my registration fees at the beginning of the year, but nothing else. Study guides? Textbooks? Anything to do with my studies? Not forthcoming. My tuition fees were required for me to return again for the next year. And the whole year he had been using it up as usual, every month. If she had wanted to, she could not. He made sure of that. And now that she had come into some money from my grandmother he wanted that too—and did get some of it. But he failed there because of a stipulation my grandmother made that the money was for me, not to him. And that was what enabled me to negotiate next year and continue—against all his plans and his wishes for me—to return to him and his belt—and whatever other thing he felt he could give me. I figured it was wise to leave soon for Cape Town without notice. There was no way I was going to let him interject with his plans. I woke up that morning with freedom in mind, no matter what Red Sea before me.

I did my best to stay calm and adhere to the routine without raising any suspicion. It was easy to remain discreet about my packing as I had brought only an overnight bag.

It was my only shot. I could not be held captive, and that was the direction it was going in. I arranged with Ree to book me a ticket for the same day, in the afternoon. He—*HE*—would be out. I quickly bathed and put on the drabbest outfit so as not to blow my cover. Then I informed Elizabeth I must leave urgently—that I had "mentioned" earlier that I won't be staying long due to "school work". I hadn't mentioned anything but hey, I learned from the best! She seemed disappointed that I had to leave, or pretended to, but as I approached the door the *HE* called! One of my distant grandmothers—supposedly Elizabeth's cousin—had blown my cover! It's hard to explain about culture. Each one to his own but with us it's like this: you don't go anywhere without telling anyone and you don't come back without greeting everyone.

This cannot be happening I thought to myself. She had bumped into him on the street and asked him to wish me safe travels for my trip that evening! You can imagine the reaction from an outwitted devil. I knew I had to dial up the little girl in me now and get to town the same way I used to—by foot. My plan was to get to the bus stop without being intercepted—I knew there was nothing malicious he would attempt to do in public.

We wouldn't want the family name tainted now, would we? Here was his last chance to prevent me from leaving, his last chance to have me under his thumb again, under his fist and under his belt. Technically he could still hold me as my guardian and prevent me by law from leaving the house—I was not yet 18 and still a minor.

The road I had travelled in my youth held many shadows for me that day. Behind every street pole, behind every bush, was a demon dog. I'm glad it was day time and the sun was out but still it felt like midnight to me. He did appear, sure enough, but too late. And loaded with sweets and chocolates. For "his lovely daughter that's going back to school". Perhaps those waiting with me at the bus stop were fooled. No doubt he was as good as ever at playing the hypocrite. But it was a sweet moment for me watching the hypocrite twitch and squirm like a toad in his skin while we waited.

The minutes must have passed like torture for him, while I was perfectly in control. And maybe then, only then, he felt a feeling he had never felt before in his life. A feeling of fear when he looked at his slave, uncaged. Who had been beaten him at his own game.

19

Access granted

It was as if time was standing still when I enrolled for my second year. I just couldn't wait to turn 18 in August 2007 and be eligible for a job on campus so I would be self-sufficient. Meanwhile, I juggled between plans to make things work. You know what I was coming out of and you know what I did not want to go back to.

To survive the next seven months was the goal. And not to be put off by whatever challenges I was facing in the lecture room. Income was now the issue. Staying alive. I had secured myself my room on campus, how was I going to pay for it? How was I to secure myself a base from which I could operate—an alternative to that thing called home that I had not experienced up to now?

How was I to make a home for myself, my own space, from which I could view the world apart from the world? These were the questions and the challenges facing me now. That load we all carry along the road toward emancipation. Most times it's in the mind. But from day to day you need to move on, it doesn't matter how you move—running—walking—limping—or crawling. Whatever you do, do not standstill. Because standing still is as good as walking backwards. Then you may as well turn around and walk back to where you came from. Walking was not an option for me, I crawled my way forward, no matter how many tangled thorns along the way—thorns that left me with scars—scars that further damaged the bruised little girl in me. I almost want to be grateful for this, it was from a place of crawling that I learned humility. It was from a lowly place that I was able to see things that those who were higher up couldn't see.

There was priceless wisdom to be found in not having all the resources I needed.

My application for student financial aid had been approved. The financial aid took care of my tuition, accommodation and came with an allowance for food, books, printing—which was bound to be depleted in no time regardless of how sparingly I used it. Half of my problems were solved, I just had to make sure I kept passing to keep the financial aid coming for next year and the next. I felt guilty for wanting more, for wanting clothes on my back, money for my hair, petty cash for printing. Was I being a spoiled brat? Those last seven months of what you can call my childhood were the longest I had to endure. No doubt the circumstances were different but that did not make it any easier. It made it more difficult in some ways. Because my environment was different and everything around me demanded a new way to cope with it. I was no longer in my native township. Rather I was in the world and the world was vain and egotistical and materialistic and image-driven and ruthlessly scornful of anything that wasn't up to your class. Rich kids all over, kids of rich parents, while I was an "orphan".

I was born towards the back end of apartheid, toward the beginning of racial desegregation, but there are other forms of that system equally ruthless and hurtful. You could have divided us there on the campus lawn into hundreds of separate little countries all with their status that prevented you from being part of the country next door. Somehow I fitted into one of these countries but really, what country was it I wanted to belong to? One where you keep your head held up high. *Chin up, princess. Daughter of the King. Consistency. Consistent to yourself. True to yourself.* I had to tell myself things like that, remind myself. I wanted to give up so badly so many times.

The mental load, the emotional load, the physical on top of it. The history of me so far, 17 going 18. And maybe now looking down from my mountain I can see more of a view. And see the kingdoms of the world. And see there is yet One I bow down to. Not a creation of His. Surviving was becoming unbearable but I had to remind myself of the why. Often in life we set goals and take actionable steps to propel us toward our desired outcome but along the way we tend to forget our why. The noise of the crowd around us and the busyness of life tends to rob us from remaining faithful to our goal.

Sometimes it's not even external systems and circumstances that get in our way but the enemy within us. How easy it is when you have travelled so far to stop and take a rest and grow complacent! We tend to forget at that moment the work that lies ahead of us. We mistake our camping site for our final destination and find ourselves settling down instead of maintaining focus and pushing on toward our finishing line. No doubt a camping site is preferable to running the race, a race that is consistently unpredictable, with no guaranteed wins. But it makes you understand why God allows us to endure situations that are unbearable, passing through prolonged seasons of excruciating pain in order to arrive at the other end. It's to build stamina, long-distance power, built-in power, to see you through. You know as an athlete you prepare yourself for the type of race you will run. You train for speed or for long distances. The hare may fly faster than the tortoise but who will win? Maintaining the load rather, maintaining forward movement, keeping yourself going, no matter what is happening around you. And never forgetting where you are coming from and where you are going and why. Which can easily happen when you take the campsite route.

It's not easy they say, from my side I can't promise much. I can promise you it is possible to get to the other side. But I can't promise you it will be easy. It doesn't matter how slow you go, as long as you keep moving. It's in between your starting point and finish line that life happens, the rest is irrelevant. Living in the moment, embracing every challenge, applying every lesson along the way, you will arrive at your final destination, rest assured.

My feeling is: if you keep avoiding those painful hardships they will have their way of catching up with you. It's called Life on Life's terms! Whoever said "a hungry stomach, an empty wallet and a broken heart can teach you life's most valuable lessons" certainly knew what they were talking about. If you have experienced one or two out of these three I bet you can attest to it.

There's a certain level of resilience and tenacity you tap into if you have been down any of these roads. You may go to University but have you been to Adversity? You may have your doctorate in philosophy, have you been to the school of hard knocks? To remain stubbornly persevering in the face of challenges while maintaining elasticity is not a skill you get taught but a skill you wilfully learn. Embrace the pain and rise above it or the pain will embrace you and drown you. Before I knew it a job advertisement poster was all over campus for a Writing Center Student Assistant.

The job description was apple crumble if you were coming from some other place far from where I was coming from. The successful candidate was to assist students in basic computer literacy skills as they typed out their assignments and getting them ready for printing. That all sounds easy but remember there was no apple crumble where I came from. Freshman here had never touched a computer before, had only seen one through the window at high school or passing by the administrator's or headmaster's office. Things like a keyboard and mouse were alien objects to me. I saw boxes and screens you call "CPU" and "monitor" but really I had no clue what they were. Computer illiteracy was a thing back then, it still is today. Not everyone has power at home or access to a laptop. Survival mode does not require computer literacy but if I was to survive in this new world I was to find a way around it.

As mischief would have it, one of the musketeers was already employed at the Writing Center and excelling at what she did. Her computer skills were dazzling to me, beyond my reach, beyond my world, her fingers flicking like lightning up and down the keys. It would feel for me like I was watching a movie, me, township girl. I dreamt of being half so good. But really it was any one of us who had gone to a private school and had computer literacy as a compulsory subject. Funny how mischief found us that way, coming from different worlds. I still have a good laugh when I think about it.

Mischief our underground gangster side that could not do things normally but must find a shortcut. And how many times has she not come to our side, this gangster, when there was no other? We pushed up a few molehills and discovered that despite your declared knowledge as a candidate you would still need to prove your computer skills by writing a test. Here was my loophole! I could apply without proven computer skills so long as I could pass the test! The devil is in the details I've heard, I don't know, God is too, I do know. True to form, she offered to steal the Student Assistant papers from the previous years. True to form, I encouraged her. I would have encouraged St Peter to steal the stockings off the Virgin Mary if it would have helped. The end justified the means, that's all I can say. The idea was for me to go through every question and practice the skills required for the test. She'd stay up at night going through the questions with me, perfecting the skills, slapping my wrist every time I skipped a critical aspect of the exercise.

It's hard not to think of her fondly now and to be grateful for the sacrifice she made for me to keep going. A little push like that in the moment can make the difference between a mountain and a molehill. The little slap on the wrist could just as well have been a pat on the back.

Off you go girl!

Mischief would not leave us there. In for a penny, in for a pound. We were, after all, sitting in the pound seats. We could always go so far, we said, as to cull the competition. Discard a few of the more impressive resumes that could potentially derail our efforts. Leaving only the average candidates, who would still make me look bad. Mischief is as mischief does. I can talk about it now because it won't cost me anything and it may make you laugh. I'm not for one second promoting the idea we should all be mischievous, only my case was different. It's not as if I had that Ivy League backing behind me. And maybe Ivy League could never have taught me anything like this anyway. I could have taught Ivy League a thing or two. Here you may have a question of conscience and because of that we did not involve our third musketeer. We knew she wouldn't approve and would probably jeopardize our mission. She was more saintly than us and less rough and rowdy—typical city girl. There's a thing, it was not all rough and rowdy in the townships, it was fun sometimes too. You were closer to the earth I guess, closer to the street. Closer to life. And you could tell that she had missed out on that. I sometimes wonder what is a godly person and what isn't. What is it to have morals and high principles and values and such? I'm inclined to believe it has more to do with your behaviour and your actions toward others. How you treat them and make them feel. Again there are class issues and what is class? What puts you in one above the other apart from your grades? I would have thought the same thing. You'd say she was a person of high morals with strict boundaries in place—operating on a high level of emotional intelligence. Finances were certainly not on her list of problems —if there was such a list. She was beyond being bothered with securing a part-time job. Call it what class you like but in that class the problems were all nice problems. A nice problem, let me explain. Like when the bell rings at the end of a lecture and you the majority rush off to queue for the computer and you the minority stroll by with a laptop under your arm and make out like it's the majority's problem. That's a nice problem. Anywho, my test day arrived and I passed as per plan. I recorded the highest mark and was hired by default.

Step one…

One small step for me, one huge step for mankind.

A prayer answered you can say.

Mission accomplished.

By hook or by crook.

I want to thank God, I want to thank everybody, even those opposed to me from the beginning. Because of them all, I was somehow here today looking at the end of my financial troubles.

But still, it was but the beginning. But the start of the next level. No time for parking off. No time for camping. I had yet to secure my position since I knew as much or less than anyone needing my assistance.

Step two…

A letter of appointment.

Perhaps it means nothing to you. But I wonder today how life would have been without it. And if all along I had not been working toward that one thing. Never knowing if I would ever arrive at it. Or if anyone would employ me. Why should they? I mean, all I was good for at that point was loading bricks and pig food. And something told me there was something about that paper that said no, I could do more than that. Even if I had to throw away a few better CV's into the trash can. Here I wonder too what a difference friends make. If without friends I could have done anything at all. Or if even one friend is all it takes to succeed. Working together I gained legitimate on-the-job training in the upcoming weeks. I'd go in with her on her shifts and she'd do the same with me—enabling me to make mistakes without our supervisor noticing. But really, what I was needing was… Ree! I had always admired his selflessness and how he went out of his way to make sure I didn't have to face more obstacles than I should and here was the proof of it. He might not have had the money to buy me a laptop but he was in a position to gain me access to one. He had gone so far as to tell his mother he needed it while it was me that needed it! He understood what was at stake here—my freedom. He saw how important computer literacy was for me to continue and not lose my job. Time was a major constraint and I was under immense pressure to get the basics right and prove I was capable. With a laptop under my arm, empowered like my Nice Problem friend, I was now able to continue my training off campus and become fully familiar with the language. In no time I was operating on autopilot and focusing on other things. I had never understood the cost of printing and photocopying for students and I still don't. Of all the places where students need support, it is here where the sharks seem to have found a market and are given free rein to feed. A student will spend his last money on printing while going hungry at home. How many times was a vetkoek all that there was between me and an empty stomach? My wages were sufficient for my printing and photocopying costs and of course I made free use of the Writing Center's resources. I'm grateful, as I say, for every contribution in my life. It's one of the reasons I feel I should also contribute. Still, no parking off. No camping. I was telling you about the classes and how the classes were divided and how money and image and style and fashion were vehicles like no BMW has ever seen. Take whatever brand you like, whatever label, there is nothing to divide people like clothing. And for someone like me who came from where—a place where there was no love even—where was

I going to now find a shoe? Me who was comfortable enough with hammy downs all my life, but now I was far away and together with this lot… There was no such thing as a mall where I came from. It was like walking into a film set. And the cars and the lights and the streets and the traffic… the consciousness of a world apart from my own that I could never belong to even if I was dressed for the part. Here I was in the university world and university was fashion conscious. And if you were not you may as well have been unconscious. But it's more about how a girl feels and how she is seen and how she is seen to be seen—by herself. It didn't matter before about crocodile shoes but now if there were shoes, well, anything but Crocs. And definitely I knew how to dress and how I wanted to look. And that of course would require more money. The next logical step for me, I figured, was to apply for a cashier role at a retail store. I could qualify for lucrative staff discounts and be the first to know about written-off stock. So said my fellow students, already employed. From my side, all I would need for my assessment was a high score in math. That, to me, was a nice kind of problem. From there I bagged my second part-time job, a job that put clothes on my back for the duration of my degree.

Step three…

How simple it seems to me to see life as a journey and a toddler taking his or her first steps. From being a baby for so long, then crawling, then talking, then… walking. No longer a baby any more but a human being. When I saw myself transcending boundaries and overcoming obstacles I couldn't help but step back and be grateful for my horrific childhood and what it taught me. It turned out what was made to work against me at the time was meant to work for me in the long run. It is from this place that I began to see my pain as a blessing. I wear my past with a badge of honour. Often times it is said that we are not our past, I say we are. We just need to be cognizant not to be bound and held back by our past, that's the difference-maker. But overlooking it is like denying the very core of our being. There wouldn't be this version of me without my past, every aspect of it remains an integral piece of the puzzle. Reflecting on my first two years of university and how I was relentlessly in survival mode, no margin for error, I learned life lessons I still carry with me as an adult—lessons about determination. There is something Bishop T.D Jakes once said that stuck with me and is applicable in every area of my life. He said when you pray and ask God for tables and chairs you will pray until kingdom come because God will give you a tree—out of which you ought to make tables and chairs. I found that profound as I realized the high likelihood of countless opportunities I must have missed because I simply didn't see the table and chairs in the tree. Notwithstanding the fact that with the tree I was given at university I was able to make a few chairs, and a table possibly, though unknowingly.

20

Choosing not to choose

There's a level of hunger you need to get a degree. Where I came from, was not only a place of no dreams as I've said, it was also a place of no inspiration, and certainly no point of reference where success was concerned. Working at the local supermarket after passing your Matric was defined as securing a good job. While becoming a clerk at the local municipality or a bank teller meant you have exceeded the standard. Needless to say, it was never a place of hopes. No wonder the late great Steve Biko had to escape the place as soon as he was born. I'm not sure if the world would have been graced with his unique vision of Black Consciousness if the grandmother of this incredibly courageous anti-apartheid activist had continued to raise him here. I want to believe she felt the greatness of her grandson in her bones and knew that our Sodom and Gomorrah would swallow his dream before it even began. And yet… here I am.

In my case, I was hungry enough not for my degree but my freedom—hungry enough to go to bed on an empty stomach. It was a small price to pay for me. The degree was merely the means toward my end—an indispensable catalyst toward acquiring my freedom.

Which may make you want to reflect on your life and ask what if you gave up too soon? What if you threw in the towel on your dreams because instead of things becoming easier, they got harder and you couldn't see your way out?

And what if every time you woke up with positivity and told yourself that things would be better they got worse instead? I had witnessed my fellow freshmen dropping out after the first semester because of the same position I was in. The only differentiator was: they had homes to go back to, and I didn't.

Then I watched pregnant bellies pop out like chickenpox all over campus. Girls from villages and towns all over the country come to throw themselves at what?

Spending their entire weekends at the campus pub instead of the study hall. The way I saw it, it was no different from where I was coming from.

And I wonder here if perhaps there was not maybe some good in a church upbringing. Perhaps there was some law I had learned, some principle.

That I couldn't just do that like they were doing. I still had something in me that said no, there is more to it than this. But I don't want to say it was a church upbringing, no. But rather the one who has taken care of me up to now, that was taking care of me then.

But the enticement of the city life that we saw on TV was now a reality and undeniably within reach. Whatever it was you wanted you could have, you had no parent to say no and no parent to watch over you.

I wonder if parents now would wonder how well their children would do, not at their studies, no, but at life. How well would they apply now the life principles they had taught their children. If they had life principles at all. Or if the children had parents. Or if it was a community thing, or a social thing or a church thing, the test for any one of them would have been how well did the product of that church, that school, that society, that community, stand against the onslaught of the world?

No doubt the world was thrown at us as we were at the world and how easy now it would have been for any one of us to "let go and let God." Only it was not God, no, but the devil. And I had enough of that. Perhaps it helped me to be watchful as a child and observant. To be on my guard always and have my eyes wide open.

Fighting for survival then was no different to fighting for survival now. I could see what was happening all around me. People dying in front of my eyes. Or disastrous betrayals of confidence, abuse of trust, resulting in scandals. The ongoing party throughout, the ongoing intoxication, the drug experimentation leading to drug addiction that popped a balloon of big dreams before they even started. I was wide awake enough to know I had to tread carefully despite the mysteriously attractive life. What kept me going along my path?

What saved me from temptation?

What ordered my steps along the way of life, a narrow way leading to life, not to destruction? God knows. But I didn't need any motivation to refrain from such allurements. Too many of my peers got entangled by giving up on the will to resist. I was not willing to take that chance because I wasn't sure if I had what it took to restrain myself. Flee temptation it is written. Avoid it in every way and form.

Choose not to. Choose not to choose, if all the choices are bad. A basket of fruit, a cake on a plate, a table of drinks, a platter of eats, choose. But you say no, I would prefer not to.

I would prefer not to choose.

Here is where friendships are put to the test. Relationships. Here is where they stand or fall. Your choice defines your friends, not your friends your choices.

Here you can see a life founded on religious instruction fails against a sense of morality. How a life raised religiously is not a life raised righteously. To be raised righteously means to make righteous decisions. And there is no difference here between a big and a small decision, they are all big decisions. And finally, you make them all by yourself with nobody to say this way or that way. You may not even need to have been raised that way—so long as you take responsibility for your own decisions. Being raised by religious folks is no strong point when at last you are faced with the world. If your training has not strengthened you inside to know who you are and know what you want, you will find you know nothing at all, and know nothing about yourself.

I saw how hypocrisy and a false sense of security failed to stand by my friends when their hour of temptation came. One drink, two drinks, all is forgotten.

How the mighty are fallen! But were they mighty to begin with? Their choices will show. The old me was back, slowly but surely, with textbooks being available. Textbooks, after all, were more of an anchor to me than any Bible. No hymn book was going to save me here. Only to get the information I needed to carry on with my life.

I was working still, away from my studies a lot, but still, my marks started improving. I passed my second and third academic years on an ascending scale. 19 years old now and my world was opening up for me.

One thing I can say at this stage, I no longer looked like where I came from. That township girl was long since put to bed. I may still have her inside me and I always will but on the outside she was now a city girl. At least that is what the mirror would tell me. And don't you think it was about time? How long had I suffered my rags! But look, another here was clothing me anew in garments as white as snow.

From the latest hairstyles to stylish handbags, I spared no budget for fashion. Nevertheless, no spendthrift. Rather searching for what would best suit me at quarter the price—Jo Borkett, Guess, Nine West,

Chuck Taylor, designer labels made cheaply available through massive staff discounts at my clothing retail job. A sense of taste you may be born with. Or you may develop it along the way. Either way I had an eye for beauty and if that is all it is, well… I was proud of the woman I had become.

Perhaps no one else remembered the three skirts, the one pair of jeans, the one pair of cargo pants I wore week in and week out in my early days.

Perhaps no one remembered the girl. But I did. And yes, Minglish was a thing of the past now. Perhaps the company is important and exposure to good literature, I don't know. My musketeers helped me and in general I picked up from where I could the art of the language, which is more like an inheritance. You are born speaking the language, I have found, and if you are not you are born again into it.

Pressing on toward my goal I applied for a third part-time job as a tutor in Management 101. Two months later I was appointed tutor-coordinator. So here I was suddenly sitting pretty as a regular student in a Master's student position.

Township-turned-city girl in her cosy consultation room supervising tutors and Masters' students! I think back on these days and wonder about what actually is possible, one can never tell. You simply throw yourself at it and see what it throws back at you.

And today I don't know what Theodore saw in me—my Management 101 lecturer—may his soul rest in peace. Leadership is a funny thing. Perhaps we are born to lead. Perhaps it is in our genes. We inherit certain qualities perhaps. And we cannot suppress those qualities. I had always been labelled a bully at school whenever leadership was required. But really, it was no bullying—I had been bullied enough in my life—only a leader, leading naturally. There would be instances where I would find myself inherently leading despite the leader being present. That instinct had taken a back seat during university—

unfamiliar territory—but appointed leader or not, I never stopped holding those around me accountable. And maybe that is all there is to be said about leadership.

A leader recognizes what job it is that needs to be done and how it is to get done. He identifies each one capable of helping him get the job done. Then he takes responsibility for the job himself. Taking responsibility for his failure also.

Then there is the matter of courage and a sense of courtesy. There was no good offending anyone you needed to get the job done. But rather through empathy and consideration of the other draw the best out of the other.

Being a radical leader himself and an uncompromising politician at heart, could these be the signs of natural leadership that Theodore saw in me?

Seeing past the insecurity? *I am not good enough* one voice would whisper in my head. *And you can't speak English the right way* another would say, only louder than the first one. The same voice that sabotaged me whenever Ree spoke English with me. I saw that as classing me, don't ask me how, but that's what insecurities do to you when you don't manage them. It's all fine and well having a meeting inside your head when you are familiar with all the voices and they are all friendly. It's those others that disturbed me. Forever trying to take me back along that road I was coming from. True enough, my accent, while exotic, impacted my speech negatively. English as a communication tool is a stumbling block for many but I wasn't going to let it dictate to me. I wasn't about to let such an opportunity go by because of insecurities unfounded and standards that are not my standards. I would speak it my way and be proud of it and add what was unique to me to the equation. But to this day, in the corporate world, because the corporate world is Eurocentric, you are taken for ignorant or stupid or lacking in intelligence for speaking with an accent. "You're from where...?" I have heard often enough.

This was far from the case with a team of professionals I met in March 2009 during an internship interview. Young, smart, black, educated, they introduced me to the corporate world. Even that sentence is not supposed to make sense—because of the one word: black. Well educated is putting it mildly, considering where some of them were coming from. Graduating Suma Cum Laude while at it. Those from South Africa had been through the University of Cape Town—counted among the best in the country, and the world. Business Science degrees, Suma Cum Laude, Cum Laudes, distinctions all, nothing less. Literally and figuratively, out of my league! My nerves played along with me that day, blinded by the intellect. Intellect, after all, was my strong point. Or so I thought. I dragged it along behind me like a reluctant shadow as I walked into the boardroom—into a realm that was way above me. I was out of my element. Listening to them I could have sworn they were all Caucasian—only that was in my mind.

The panel boasted nine investment professionals in all: five Africans, three Caucasians and one Indian. Of the nine only one was female and she was my colour. *Yes!* Then they began talking and my eyes flicked from one to the other in disbelief. My ears could tell no colour. I could tell no African or Caucasian or Indian from the other.

It was like I had landed on a new planet, a new world where all the things from the old one were gone. Here were human beings starting over again from what they were in the beginning. Like God had simply set back the clock and said "here, let's start again with a new lot here in the boardroom. Eve, your turn to talk."

Talk about blown away. Impressed. Impressed how? I mean impressed emotionally.

I mean impressed like when one makes an impression of one's self on another. Like when you impress your head on a gold coin so it stands proud and everyone says Hail Caesar.

I was impressed. But it wasn't just the speech, or the language, or the tongue, or any other thing. Where was English now? Who cared? But the respect, the kindness, the courtesy, the humility they demonstrated. There now was the language. The love language. The basic human decency language of basic human respect. Not once did they jump to correct my pronunciation or pretend like they hadn't understood what was coming from my mouth. It was like they had been there before in those internment shoes answering to arrogant pricks.

It was only later when I started my internship and was one of them and was shown the list of candidates I was up against that day that I saw how out of my league I had actually been.

Let's just say I'm glad I only saw that short-list afterwards. To know that I had a 1:50 chance to be selected would have totally thrown me off.

I can't help but think how many chances we miss in life because we assume we are not the right person for the job. Or we are underqualified.

Or don't have what it takes. Not the right skin colour. Or the right accent. Appropriate age. Required gender, etc—you'll find many more if you carry on looking for them.

And before we accuse the system of discrimination let's triple-check that we are not guilty of self-discrimination! Sometimes the universe has a way of sniffing and picking up when what we do or say is misaligned with what we think.

You may apply for a job just for the sake of ticking the box but deep down you have already fed yourself the lie that you are not going to win.

If you apply concluding that you're not going to get the job, why apply from the onset? I say this now but I must confess, I didn't know all this when I applied for the internship role at that asset management boutique. Where is the fun in living with guarantees in life? Is it not the unpredictability of life that makes it worth living? I am grateful to God for making Theodore believe in me. From that belief, I was able to trust myself to apply for the internship role even if I didn't meet the "outstanding academic record" description. "Do you care explaining your average marks on the core subjects while you have good marks on the soft subjects?" said one of the directors, his blue-eyed gaze giving me no time for an excuse. I can't remember how I answered that one but I don't think he was impressed. If he was, he was not convinced. I remember that part because he kept tapping his shoes and fiddling with the pen behind his ear.

It must have been a Friday because the CEO at one point asked me to sing for them during the interview, claiming it's a casual day! "Hell no!" I said, bursting into spontaneous laughter. I couldn't sing to save my life and there was no way I was going to let them enjoy their drinks later mimicking my performance in my absence. From then on everyone was laughing throughout the interview and I remember the grins on the faces—like they knew.

To be or not to be. To choose or not to choose. To be a man, they say, is not easy. To be a man is to make a decision. I don't know. I'm not a man. All I know is, I know what I wanted. And I know what I didn't want. And I wasn't going to choose to settle for anything less.

V

Part Five

Freedom is a bloody pursuit

21

Uncharted territory

Back to reality check. I knew that escaping from my hellish prison was only an interim solution to my dilemma. I had to settle on a permanent solution. Just because I was away from my step-father monster and my loveless, toxic mother didn't mean I was not a prisoner. I had to face this hard truth. Visiting for holidays in December made me ask myself questions I wasn't ready for. How am I different from Elizabeth? What if I end up being a prisoner like Elizabeth for the rest of my life? Why am I feeling like a hypocrite, playing happy families? I couldn't answer any of those, but I was at least asking.

Is this the life I truly wanted? If not, where do I begin cutting my ties? Where would I begin taking on a beast? Do I have it in me to walk away and never look back? Is there such a thing as the "right time" for what I know needs to be done? Am I ready for the backlash and judgment from the world? It was hurtful enough to know that I didn't belong but detaching myself felt paradoxically painful. I knew I didn't have the physical strength it took to stand up to my step-father and I also knew that two could play that game. Just because I beat him at his own game the last time didn't guarantee me any future victories. I was still in a precarious situation! I remained confused and conflicted, beginning to feel sorry for what my decision would do to Elizabeth, feeling guilty for leaving her at the mercy of a monster. I thought if I was out of the picture she would be tormented and tortured in my place. There was a part of me that chose to believe that she was as much of a victim as I was. I had to wake up and see things for what they were and grapple with it—she might not have executed the bloody brutality I had to endure but she had no desire to protect me. Not only that but no one forced her not to buy her teenage daughter sanitary pads every time she got a pack for herself. She was never moved to see me using a cloth for my menstrual flow—instead, she was happy to provide me with more cloth. I was never worthy enough for anything—certainly not worth enough to spend money on.

I had to prepare myself ahead of time for what was to come. That included ignoring my step-father's pathetic calls. He used to call me to "check-up" on me, something he didn't even know the meaning of. I knew ignoring his calls would unsettle him—while setting the tone for me.

Over the winter break, I took the road home again knowing that I would not stay longer than five days and that it would be my last time seeing them. I experienced the same feelings as before as the bus got closer to my destination, only this time I had Ree, I was sure about that part.

Six months can make a difference. On top of the previous year, it made twice the difference, maybe four times, who's counting? Being away from him was what made me stronger. And I was coming back with strength. I arrived home and grew restless quickly with no action. My mission was not to sit back and wait for something to happen—as if nothing had changed.

Today was the day.

Poke the bear. Poke in turn where you have been poked.

I've told you about his obsession with my hair and covering my face. Anything to do with my hair was to do with him. I would have to ask his permission. Consult him before I did anything with it. As if it was not a part of me and sprung from out of my scalp. So I went to town to get my hair done the way I wanted to, without asking permission. I know it sounds weird but we were not allowed to even plait our hair without his blessing—that's how much of a control freak he was. And being controlled angered me more than the physical abuse. It made me feel like a caged animal. Perhaps that was the last straw, I don't know. Domination comes in so many little ways. To deny him now that territory he had gained, that he had made himself the lord and master of, was perhaps the place I needed to get to. To be in control or not be in control? That was the question.

I opened the front door looking good, and I knew it. We use the word breathtaking a lot, do we know what it means? To me it was the look on her face when she saw me, the breath gone out of her. "What have you done?" Elizabeth said, trembling.

I guess she was trying to say "breathtaking" but had no breath to say it. "You love getting into trouble, don't you?" she said. While running towards the street-facing windows to check if her husband was not around. "I am ready for him!" I said, without thinking. It was at that moment that I knew I was ready. I didn't have to schedule my readiness: my mind and body had taken over. That moment alone was victorious for me, to finally say those words unrehearsed. I felt power retrieved! I was strengthened by forces I could not describe. Suddenly it dawned on me: all I needed to do all this time was make a decision and stick to it. Then, as if to test me, the beast appeared at the front door! It was an ambush no doubt but here's the thing, it didn't matter to me. My mind and body were prepared and it seemed like my soul was ready to join them. He took one quick look at my hair and turned away as if he had not seen me. The whole evening he didn't say anything. I waited and waited until sleep time, but nothing.

Strike one.

The silence continued the next day. No mention of my hair. No mention of hairdressers. No mention of anything at all that was different from what it was before. The next day dawns, what date was that? It should have been recorded in history. The day I had been waiting for. We were all sitting in the kitchen with Elizabeth preparing supper. He left the table and came back with a piece of paper and a pen. It will go down on the same day as the first day we engaged in dialogue.

"How is school?"

"School is fine."

"Do you have friends?"

"I do have friends."

"I am thinking of going back with you when you go back to school. So I can ask around about your behaviour and observe the kind of friends you have." That right there unleashed something in me I didn't know how to suppress. Like I said now, these kinds of control freak tactics infuriated me. It was in these moments that I could have killed him with my bare hands. The abuse I could take indefinitely but the control freak let loose my own devil. What does it take, exactly, for you to reach your boiling point? Surely each one of us has our limits. And it may be necessary, at last, for each one to arrive there. It's hard for me to explain what happened next or try to describe what followed. It was as if I had my own devil also and the devil had found his match. The blood under pressure inside of me seemed to be searching for an outlet through my skin. It pumped along the length of my nose and my knees were shaking uncontrollably. Have you ever been hungry for blood? Bloodthirsty? I was! I kept looking at the knives that Elizabeth was using for chopping vegetables on the kitchen counter. I looked back at his neck and knew I'd have to be a butcher to do the job properly—like you would a pig or a goat. That's what I wanted for him in that moment. I was wearing a red Disney sweater with a hood covering my head. Under the hood I plotted new ways to kill him. I had failed once as a pre-teen, I was old enough now to succeed.

"What's wrong?"

"Nothing."

"Are you on drugs?"

"I'm not on drugs."

To be fair, you too would have thought I was on drugs. I sat with both feet curled beneath me and hugging my legs and rocking back and forth in an attempt to contain my fury. "How do you spend your food allowance from your student loan?" he said, as to his former slave. "I want you to write down the price of everything you buy from Mondays to Sundays." He no doubt had no idea what he was doing. He took me from devil to something else I don't know. A weird sound like a trapped dragon came out from inside of me. I was no longer in control, the traumatized girl was travelling through time and revisiting every brutal beating and striking I'd ever received for nothing.

Still, no explosion. No outward manifestation of rage. Only a strange kind of dragon tear that denied grief and any hurt and pain that ever was. But my eyes were busy. My brain. Furiously calculating. I saw a shopping bag I could possibly use for a murder weapon. But he was against the wall, I'd need to be behind him and have room to move around for me to suffocate him to death. My dragon sounds got louder. I was surely no longer myself. I could no longer look him in the eye, what I could not control in me had taken over. "It's like I've always known," he said to Elizabeth. "She hates me. These are tears of hatred. Listen carefully. She's at it again!" He abruptly stood up from the table and threw his chair aside. For the first time I wasn't afraid.

"Look at me! Why are you crying?"

But before I could attempt a reply he let fly a fist.

That was the only way to keep me quiet he said.

To shut my mouth.

Strike two.

The strange groaning continued, deep down, from where a dog growls. One of us had to die that night, if it was him or me was secondary. I feared no dying, for where I was I was dying already—a slow painful death of being his prisoner. I knew there was a point when I didn't want to die in his hands but I didn't care any more. What mattered to me was dying in the fight for my freedom—fighting the man no man up to then had had the courage to fight.

Uncharted territory.

He punched me a second time, in the ribs, using all his power.

No part of me screamed.

No part of me begged forgiveness—the pain only served to empower me.

The fact he had punched me like he was punching a man showed me something more: he saw me as something to be feared. Feared for courage maybe, to resist, if nothing else. Regardless of punches to the face and ribs. Instead of backing off or standing down or hiding behind the kitchen chairs I stood my ground and growled even harder. Then the animal inside me, whatever it was, the creature, the spirit, the original thing we are without body or soul, found a voice. With all the years of my life behind it, for every beating, for every punch to the face and body, for every belting, for every belt buckle, for every weapon designed to kill and steal and destroy, for every lie, I unpacked my truth.

"I HATE YOU!" I screamed—and my voice was unearthly.

"I HATE YOU, YOU DOG!"

Into his face, into his eyes, into his teeth and down his throat—I poured every decibel of my hate.

He stood frozen in place, rooted to the spot, transfixed. His world had stopped and his heart stood still. He had not seen that coming. He punched me a third time, to the face, but he was finished. I had taken his best and now it was my turn. I rolled up my sleeves in reply, opened my arms, stretched out my hands like a cat, ready to fight. "I dare you to give it your best shot," I said—anticipating his fourth punch. "Because it will be your last."

I was ready to meet my maker. I couldn't tell the difference between the red lines on my white pants and the blood from my face but I was not going to go down without a fight. And I was certainly not going to let him stop when it suited him. Not this time. I had the kitchen chair in my hands, a weapon. How many weapons through the ages had he taken to me? How many times his belt, his boots, his bare hands? After all, a coward is a coward, a bully, a bully. We give them their power and we give them their ground. Before him stood someone he did not know, something he could not see. Someone fearless, fearful, he did not know. I wonder if God at that moment or His angels did not stand by me. Or all the women of all ages, women that were mothers to me. I wonder if Eve was not there, the mother of all creation. And all her daughters were with me there to send the devil to damnation. If behind me he did not see a flaming sword, or if it was just me, transfigured in some way into something he could not look at. He ran as a coward will, in terror, out the kitchen, into his room.

He ran from a woman.

And a woman would live to tell the tale.

A woman is a strange thing, a woman who cries for love. A woman who can cry for freedom also and for victory from above. I may not have thrown any punches or chairs—I may not have cut off his head—but I was the last man standing.

Strike three.

Sunday again, the next day, like the world was shiny and new.

It started with a humble request. Could I please skip church?

He'd make my apologies he said, hanging the friendliest smile from the friendliest dial—one I had never witnessed before. All it took was my craziness to believe I could overthrow a giant, and the mental strength to put that craziness into action. When they came back from church I was dressed to go, ready to leave for Cape Town. "I'll walk myself down" I said, leaving the dust behind me. I never looked back.

22

The final lap

My final year, you can say, was my final lap. I'd been running a long time. Since I was born. At full pace. Maybe there is something important to consider there. A long-distance runner does not run at full pace. He paces himself to cover the distance. No doubt he could run forever if he was only pacing himself. But mine had been the 100 meters from the beginning. And I was still running it. The way I've been telling this story. I tell it as it comes. I have given my earliest memories but I haven't tried even to tell it in one long story from start to finish. I have told it in short bursts of fury, which is the way my life was. I'm still running my race and the pace is still furious. Having qualified for an internship I now needed to divide my time between work and studies. Some days I would work half day, others full day, depending on my timetable. I was travelling between home and campus, campus and work, work and campus, campus and home again—a logistical nightmare. Tygerberg—Bellville—UWC Campus. UWC Campus—Bellville—Claremont. Claremont—Bellville—UWC Campus. UWC Campus—Bellville—Tygerberg. That was more or less what my day looked like. And Cape Town was thrown in when it was a train that was

171

needed. And waiting as long as it took for the train. Or the next train. Because the one you were waiting for was cancelled. Geographically the areas were not so far apart but to get there involved a transport system that took more time away from the table than there was a table. Miss the university shuttle and you were with the taxis. Miss the taxis you were with the trains. Miss the trains you were on the street. And from there you could have gone anywhere, you would not have been missed. And driving me regardless of my words at the interview: "I'm hungry for this opportunity, I'll do whatever it takes."

I sometimes wonder what a human being is capable of. How far you can take him if you push him hard enough. I wonder if we know anything about what is inside us and how we work. If we may yet find that we do things we never thought we could be capable of. And the Designer watches to see what is it we can still do that He knows we can do but we don't. Then again, there are people He sends your way. To show you a thing or two. And I wonder if these people are not part of His creation process. I met such a person during my internship and up to today, she will still not take credit. Probably that's the best thing about people He sends your way. On the job, I was exposed to the practical side of investments.

Concepts I used to find complex and difficult to comprehend in lecture halls were suddenly made easy as she helped me bridge my theoretical knowledge with practical skills. I was no longer working with case studies but with real-life situations—a thrilling experience for any investment professional. She walked the extra mile by taking me to investment expos and conferences. I would watch her tearing down the big guns across the table, making them eat their words. By her presence alone, by her aura, she could drive a meeting and end it as quickly. She would go into each meeting well prepared and ready for anything. She was young and female and deadly—leaving her male counterparts gasping for air or lunging for escape hatches. "Ahem…"

(clearing their throats in embarrassment) "… it was a pleasure meeting you…." I would lose myself in her voice—a safe place where I could float along without a worry in the world—a voice to control and to rule and to take charge of whatever male-dominated culture it was. No doubt she was in charge of herself and control of herself and for that reason, she was in charge and control of the meetings. The lion may make as much noise as he likes, we all know he is a lion. But the lioness will quietly get on with the job and lay food on the table. There was something about her I liked, something about her I recognised in myself—there is no use in denying it. There was no use being anything else.

"I want to be like her!" I told myself. Talking of food on the table, she taught me how to use a fork and knife. And before you go thinking township girl I'm not talking about those mass-produced monstrosities you find in the average kitchen drawer. I'm talking finely fashioned knives, finely crafted, delicate and silvery, elvish in their beauty—some with hooks and weird shapes and pointy ends. I've tackled food from every angle, from every quarter of the dinner plate. I've tackled meat, I've tackled fish, I've tackled whatever the artist has to offer. She introduced me to business etiquette and business integrity—the foundation stones for building the mining company we conceived of and brought to fruition years later.

"Do you know who you're talking to?" he said. It started like that, the meeting. We were there for due diligence, looking to secure a multi-million Rand asset. "I'm a retired financial director" he went on.

"I have an MBA from Cambridge University. I've been on TV. You must have seen me."

The "been on TV" part was what got to me. I mean, I found it funny. It was hard for me now not to burst out laughing like I had done that day when they had asked me to sing a song. Hell no! It's almost like he was advertising himself on a box of Corn Flakes. Or promoting himself for a spot on an Omo commercial. We waited patiently for him to finish. "…you're a Mickey Mouse company. Nobody knows you…" By this time I was fuming. You'll know I never was a willing participant in being bullied or assaulted. But isn't this what our training is for? And isn't this, perhaps, what all the ordeal was about? To prepare me for this kind of abuse? And to provide me with weapons to deal with it? And to send it straight back to hell, from whence it comes? Again, it was fortunate for me to have my partner at my side. It helped to have one who understood exactly how I was feeling and who was asking me not to betray my feelings. His hand on my lap was all I needed, a gentle reminder, an assurance, why we were here. It mattered less all of a sudden about the man across the table and what he was saying. From then on I was OK, I knew we had this. I have often wondered about when someone laughs or when someone smiles. When someone laughs or smiles in the way I did that day, if they should rather not worry. I smiled while I listened to my antagonist, formulating my response. I smiled, drawing from my inspiration, who knew exactly how to downsize bullies and chauvinists. I smiled with humility and dignity, without getting anywhere near emotional. Put it this way, at the end of the meeting, the old man politely pulled me aside and asked for a job. Yes! From me! A Mickey Mouse nobody! No doubt I'm no prizefighter. No doubt I'm slight and slender. No doubt I have no deep strong voice. But I've got my smile. And whatever goes behind that smile. I'm still smiling. Mentorship doesn't have to be formalized and structured—it's the small things that count. You just have to open your heart to give what you can, the best way you know how. You never know the impact you will have on someone else's life—an impact that will change someone's life forever—the way my life was changed. Success is contagious. Since her success was possible, my success was possible. I too could do it. I too would do it. I would do it because she did it. Because she could do it and I could do it. Funeka still refuses to acknowledge herself as my mentor. Perhaps she is right, she has been more than that. She has been a sister, an elder sister, to help a younger sister out. When she needed to get to her interviews. And had no bus fare. She was a friend when I needed one, inviting me out for lunch when I was struggling still, unemployed, after graduating. Apart from Ree, she was my biggest cheerleader. She was and still is, one-of-a-kind. Graduating at 20 I can easily recite the text she sent to my old Nokia: *Congratulations on your graduation dear Asa. I have no doubt that you will make an overwhelming success of your career. Love, Funeka.* When I wanted to give up on looking for a job I went back to that text. I had to succeed because apparently I was capable. I couldn't settle for anything less. I had a tribe rooting for me. I had to finish the final lap.

23

Knockout

In boxing, they say it's the punch you don't see coming that knocks you out! In the wider world, the reality we ignore or deny is the one that weakens our most impassioned efforts toward improvement. Just when I was beginning to feel I had everything under control, I had to learn the hard way just how imbalanced my reality was. I'm not sure what we can call it. A system shut down maybe. A system overloaded. Too much, for too long. I had endured too much over too long a period. On top of my childhood trauma came my adult trauma and I wonder if they were not all the same, one thing happening to one person and it all just catching up with that person. For all my life I had been running, and now whatever it was I was running from had caught up with me. But still, that is not what you call it. There is no name for it. I've come to wonder just what the human being is, just what is the machine, the construct, the creation that we are. If you can say you are mind or heart or body or soul, or all of those, I don't know. But somewhere among this lot, something was not working so well. And the whole lot said enough. It's all fine and well when one part shuts down and says enough—the other parts keep going. But really, what point in moving on in automation when part of you is being left behind? I don't know how else to explain it. We want all of us on board but one of us is saying *no, not me, no longer. I'm outta here.* Less than two months to go before finishing my studies, a degree waiting, the golden fleece, my laurel wreath, crowning me king of my conquerors. All that I had ever dreamt of in life to get me out, to get me up—to get me away from under the heel of my devil enemy—now caught up with me.

Snatching at my heel, tripping me up, throwing me down, my race run, my effort expended, my long road to freedom cut short at the finishing tape.

True I was talking about a race, a fight, had I not been running, fighting, for my life? But this hand comes from nowhere, this sucker punch, and I'm down on the canvas and the ref is beginning his count.

One...

All the parts of me, KO, knocked out, knocked down, off my feet, flat on my back, my head spinning, my world collapsed around me. Any prizefighter would know what I was feeling then. And here this voice, this end of all voices, the last voice you will ever hear, counting you out.

Two...

Or counting you in.

Three...If you can get back on your feet again. The subconscious world has a strange way of finding you, of communicating to you all is not well. You may call them dreams, you may call them nightmares, I'm not sure what they are, only they are real and they have a message for you. Outside of yourself, or inside of yourself, or apart from yourself, is still another world that talks to you. There is another life happening there. And this life remembers everything. And brings it back to you from time to time to show something to you. Are you in denial? Your subconscious world will tell you. Are you in pain? It will let you know. Are you traumatized? It will show you the reasons why.

They came like an ongoing roll of lighted pictures, scenes from my life, from my distant childhood. Distant? No. Very much with me still and running the race as fast as I was running. I could never outrun those images as I could never outrun that devil forever on my heels and picking up stones along the way to hurl at me. Would I ever escape my past? Could I ever escape it? Did I think there was a place where it could not find me? Where *he* could not find me? That was the feeling if I could put any feeling to it at all. That all my worst nightmares, all I had done to escape them, to get away from them, were with me still. Oh God…. no. Not back to that place again.

System shut down.

It means everything just stops working. Here you are the machine on autopilot doing what machines do—you don't need to feel. The brain is in charge, the Central Processing Unit, you are but the soldier carrying out orders. You do not think for yourself, neither do you feel, you do what soldiers do till the mission is accomplished. You take orders, you don't question orders. After all, where are you going? And how do you expect to get there? By stopping by the way and thinking for yourself? But there must be a time for that, surely. There must be a time for yourself. When you sit down and say enough. This race is not going anywhere. Not like this. I need to sit down and ask myself a few questions. What the hell just happened here? What has my life been about up to now? No doubt in long-distance running there is never a time to just stop and take a rest. A camping site. But really, if the race you are running is getting you nowhere, better to stop and ask why. Because this sure ain't doing you any good, girl. That much is obvious. Maybe if you were raised with a lot of love and no fear it would be different. But up to now, there had been no love and it was only fear. And fear was my devil. Either way, it could not have come at a worse time. Finals in a week. And here I am shutting down, experiencing what the professionals call a mental breakdown. Fellow traveller, will you take a seat with me? Will you sit down for a second and process this with me? It had happened to me before. There were warning signs. A moment when sitting down for my paper I just could not remember anything. Not even my student number. Which I still know now by heart. But at that moment, back then, before the examiner, I could remember nothing. My system shut down. My body machine saying no. My CPU section goes into pause mode, pause a moment, pause the game. And autopilot asking who the hell have I still got here to go on with? I'm trying to put down how it feels to be in this place where you have a system shut down. I want people to recognize the signs. See it coming. Are you pushing yourself too hard? Too long? Been pushing yourself more than you should push yourself? It's going to catch up with you. See it coming, know it is coming. Be prepared when at last it comes. And you do not get floored with a sucker punch. No doubt I was losing my mind. At least that is what it felt like. Losing control. Losing yourself. Who was I any more? Who was doing my thinking for me? Not me. Like a zombie, I moved forward, or stood still, or moved backwards, or did whatever the next one was going to tell me. No doubt I was a mental patient. No doubt I needed someone to lead me by the hand. Me who had always been so independent. Looking to absolutely nobody. Because I couldn't afford to. It's difficult for me to be talking about this. Why? Because I don't want to go back there. I don't want to go back to that moment. It's still too close to me and here I am finding whatever courage is still left to me to continue telling you about it no matter what. It felt like my world was standing still. But the real world carried on. And you know, maybe it is good that it did. Life must go on like a river goes on. Or you must find yourself a parking place along the bank. No doubt here was my time for a camping site. *Rest up a while girl. Let the river go by.* But still, it felt like to me if I stopped I would disappear down a black hole. I would just be swallowed up into nothingness and cease to exist. My whole life, whatever it was, was gone. My whole life ahead was no longer a life. The sinkhole was at my feet and I was about to be swallowed up forever. In a situation like that, it helps to have some kind of a line, anything—even a line of coke. No, I will never say that, but you know what I mean. Anything to keep you going. Anything to stop you from being swallowed up and going under. I had lost my moorings before. I had felt my mind slipping away with me. I had felt myself losing control and floating in a world where I no longer existed as an entity but as a molecule. Some kind of space atom that existed as a space atom and that is all. There's one thing I believe I am. I believe I am a soul. And one thing I don't want to be is a lost soul. Focus: real world. I had been given study leave at work and was due back to complete my internship immediately after exams. *No one cares about your problems* I heard my devil saying. I needed professional help fast. I was losing my mind. Knowing the horror of losing your mind, I do not use the phrase lightly. Tell me something, let me ask you, what do you do when you are in that place?

What is it you can do to help yourself?

What are you, who are you, to say *no worries? I can handle this. I can manage this. I can get through it.* I couldn't. I couldn't handle it. I couldn't manage it. And I couldn't get myself through it. I needed help. I'm independent, always have been. But sometimes you need to depend on somebody. And maybe that's the lesson. Or I don't know what the hell the lesson is. Needless to say I was incapacitated for sitting for my final exams and because I couldn't prove it to the exam board I had to drop out—as in, abandon my studies. Ree to the rescue, Jesus, whoever. He had his own exams to prepare for—was busy with his own future—but I could see, by the look on his face, I was in just so much trouble as I imagined.

Right now I'm talking to you about it but back then I was still in denial. *Oh, this is not happening to me. There's nothing wrong.* But looking at him looking at me that way I knew there was. And he was as worried about me as I should have been worried about myself. Here's a point. Mirrors. You may go to the mirror to see how beautiful you are. Or so ugly. You may consult the mirror like the witch in Snow White. But the mirror can only lie. It's made that way, to tell you the opposite of what you see with your own eyes. To get a real mirror you need to look into the eyes of someone you love. And who loves you enough to tell you the truth. *I'm surrendering here. I'm in his hands. I'm no longer in control. Somebody is going to take me forward from here.*

Something had to be done! Fast! But how? I had no cash for a start—not for a psychologist or a psychiatrist. I had no medical aid cover. What we did have was a psychologist on campus. Ree negotiated an appointment for me to be seen urgently. I was to go alone—he had an exam on that day—no hiding behind him or looking for a pillar to hang onto. Weak I was, as weak as I ever was in my life. And here I was, whatever hope was left, pinned on a psychologist. What was going on in my mind as I sat there in that waiting room, I'm trying to remember. What was going on in my heart? In me? Who was me? Who was I? And where were we going? And what was I doing here? Maybe there's a time for neutral gear. Just stay out of gear for a while and idling. Was it really as bad as this? That I had ended up at a psychologist? A shrink? And some head doctor was somehow going to fix me up? Set me straight? And I'd continue as if nothing had ever happened? I just don't know. I just don't know if problems like this can be fixed with a few sessions talking to somebody and have them tell you stuff. Surely it takes the rest of your life to work through your problems if your whole life went into it? Or do you just slip some pills and hope for the best? I was called in some time later, can't remember how long, the rest of the details are blank. I remember being in the consultation room with someone who seemed to know what she was doing. At least, if hypnotists know what they are doing. "I think you're just anxious about exams" she said, looking for more information, I think, in my eyes. "It's quite normal to suffer from anxiety during this time" she droned on. Right there, right then, I could have given her the reaction she was looking for. Right then I could have come alive all of a sudden and jumped off my chair and jumped over the desk and throttled her quietly while she was looking still into my eyes. I wonder then what she would have seen—an anxious person stressed out by exams or all of hell that I had endured that she somehow could not see.

Trauma? No.

Abused? No.

Suffering? No.

Ongoing abuse? No.

A history of all these, and a future dictated to by these? No. It was like nothing had ever happened in my life and there was never any reason for me to be sitting there in that chair.

Spoiled brat.

"Unfortunately I can't help you" she said. "As there is nothing wrong with you." The words came from a far place, as far back as where I was coming from. Like a spell reaching you from some place you know nothing of, from some dark star that somehow governed your life from far out in the galaxy. *Here you end your road* it said. *From here on, no further. Your life is now my life and your destiny my destiny.* I had never known that words could have such power, like words over a grave. I felt I was being buried alive and here was my epitaph. I became numb, as if she had injected me with some kind of anaesthetic. Her words fell as a distant echo—distorted amplifications from a distant star. "The end of the road" we say. The end of the road for me. Long road to nothing. Nothing at all. Only a black hole and a black void and a black nothingness. My eyes, I think, if she had seen what I was feeling, what lay before me for my soul, would have shown her. A dark and alien and cold wilderness far out from here, far out in the vacuum of space. *Not here at all* they would have told her. *Not here at all.* Nevertheless the part of me I call the professional would not quit. Still asking questions. Still reasoning. Still rationalizing. Still pressing on toward my goal. It's a formidable thing. Like some kind of indomitable terminator I still could not relinquish my quest. Some programmed brain inside me still operated regardless. It was no longer a path of faith or belief I was on but the path of determination. And I wonder at last if that may not be as powerful as anything there is on earth. But here I was, on earth. A vessel of clay, flesh and blood, breakable, expendable, with no medical certification to prove my incapacitated state to the examination board. It was over! My sacrifices, my tears, my struggle, my years, a four-year degree, an internship, my way out of the drain back down the drain in a split second! Oh, if we could but be that single thing, a professional! If only we did that one thing right and forgot about everything else! If a psychologist could but be a psychologist and not some stargazing witch looking for loopholes into the industry! Here my life landed on her desk and she took it and crumpled it up and tossed it into the waste paper basket. Like she had done with so many others. What a mess I was in! What a mess! But here again, someone else comes to the party. Someone else takes over. And I have no problem saying that independence has its place and it is very important but upon some point you are going to have to depend on somebody. And God made it that way. Ree was thinking on his feet. He was seeing what I was not seeing. Maybe what everyone was seeing but me. My machine man didn't see any of these things. My machine man was not human. Never was. He came up with a "plan" as they say, a plan that could have got him into a lot of trouble. He was willing to take that chance he said. And I wonder what else a man is for, if a man is in love and he sees something worth more than anything else there is around. The pearl of great price I was not, no doubt, neither was I anybody's black diamond, I was black all by myself and bright and shiny before that. Only I was someone he cared for, and I wonder what diamond or pearl can compare to that? And to think how young he was, how supposedly irresponsible, how selfish, etc—how inconsiderate the majority can be. I mean, what was it at that point that we had together? What future was it we were working on? More likely it was a day to day affair whereby we would see from one day to the next how it would work out. There was no idea here of long-term or commitment or anything like marriage, only mutual company and being together for the moment. We were both as free and easy to cut loose any time we wanted. Truth be told, he had no reason to stay. He had no reason to waste his time on a messed up girl while he could be out there enjoying his youth. He didn't deserve to be mixing himself up in my baggage and finding himself carrying my burden. But that's who he was and that's who he still is: one-of-a-kind. Ree, I have said, came from a different home to mine. A different background. Here there was support where I had no support, shelter where I had no shelter, a secure and stable family base and a sense of well-being and security that I could not even dream of because I never knew such a thing existed. He came with his own world that was not my world but somehow our worlds collided. And it has never been the same for either of us again is all I can say. So, Ree had his mother. Like I did, but different. She had medical aid, for instance. And being a dependent of hers, with his sister, the plan was to speak to her to allow me to get professional treatment in his sister's name. His angle was forfeiture, the funds were readily available, no one had to pay anything, they would forfeit the funds anyway if we did not use them. Perhaps this sounds mischievous again but really… this was survival. The option was for me to get treatment or to book myself into an asylum. What support at this stage could I expect from anybody at home? What mother now was going to come to my rescue? But Ree took it upon himself to do what he could do and if it was the wrong thing, he didn't care. As he made clear, he would take his chances. What money was it anyway that was being paid month by month into the medical aid? Still, he took no chances to ensure when I went in that day his sister was not going in for anything. That would have led to a red flag and a potential fraud case. Everyone came to the party, no questions asked. Ree was honest with the psychologist and she agreed to take me on for a couple of sessions.

So at last I ended up in a place where I could get help. At least, a place where I could begin to get help. And also find a way to carry on with my life. And have my career back on track. But really, the career was secondary. It was my mental health first. The psychologist now on duty I can call a psychologist. I'm not sure at all what the other one was. Surely she was no help to me. But this one was. And I want to say she was coming from a different place to me, a different culture, a different way of being raised—that much was immediately obvious to me. For a start there was not that local thing of "take whatever hell is landed on you and embrace it like a man." *No matter what abuse, no matter what ongoing nightmare, this is the African way, we are used to it. Family first, culture, etc. There's no denying your culture. No fighting it either. And certainly, no disowning it.* This goes deep because for any African his identity is wrapped up in his culture and the ongoing pressure he feels to conform to his culture and not go against it is immense. After all, he would not want to displease the elders, would he? And then there are *abaphantsi*—the ancestors—to consider. So, being a man, a woman, born into this culture, but not feeling as if I belonged to it, it stood against me. And I need only mention one word here— family—to explain what I mean. Did I have any family? Did I have anything at all like family? Or just a collection of people out to destroy me at every opportunity? That, surely, is not family. This is what my psychologist explained to me. And that goes deep because you surely are the product of your family. And surely your culture plays an important role in how you are formed and how you assume your identity. But my own had made me hate myself rather and be in fear of any other thing I must learn along the way. And that was behind some of my trauma that must finally catch up with me, no matter what. Staying away from my family then was the solution. *Cut all ties. Emotionally you cannot benefit there. Emotionally you need to protect yourself. No more of that. That will kill you. Or drive you insane. Or drive you to any kind of substance that will provide an escape route.* And is that not the danger for us all? To find something to dull the pain, to anaesthetize it? And I wonder if the majority of us are not in this place where we run to something, anything, to escape it. To church even. At last we were beginning to talk about these things. At last these things were coming to the light. The damage I had suffered from my trauma was quite severe, she said. It's hard to put it into words. I was reliving my childhood experiences, my body was going through the same pain I went through back then. I say my body, I mean the flesh and blood machine with all the connections to heart and soul and mind and memory. I suppose that's why they call it a nervous breakdown. It's all the links between that say *enough, overload.* And they simply stop talking to each other. We may talk also about pain but that really does not cover it. Let us talk about hurt and damage and stress and tension and fear and anxiety and all of it drawn out along a line of infinity that could never break but was always on the point of breaking. You can tune a steel string to however high you want it to sound, you can wind that string till it sings like a harp, I wonder if it was not me when the harpist plucked me with his index finger—so highly strung there was hardly a noise to come out of me and what noise there was nobody wanted to hear or could hear. The pain I used to feel as a child was that kind of pain, a silent invisible pain that nobody could register. A note more like it, from a tuning fork, passing through eardrum and blood vessel and bone matter and brain matter—discerning even the thoughts and intents of the heart. Either way, whatever hell it was I had to endure as a child came knocking at my door uninvited— unannounced—to claim a spot inside of me. They were not there for a meet and greet or a quick visit either, and they certainly didn't ask for my approval, they were clearly there to stay. I was powerless and not in control any more—regardless of how strong or brave I thought I was. That steel-stringed prong was the overriding note, overriding everything. A silver line with no silver lining, a silvery spiralling coil unwinding—twisting me out of control. And I still can't pinpoint what triggered me when it triggered me— or how it triggered me. The thing about trauma is, it's so mystically connected to triggers that you don't have to be aware and conscious for you to be triggered. Your trauma is so powerful that it is able to sniff and recognize your triggers from a distance—while it is business as usual for you.

So, everything had stopped. Everything on hold. My life. My career. My future. All three so intricately wrapped in the other. And what options? What to turn to? Who to turn to? It was not in my nature to look to a man. Or to a woman either. Certainly, I had not been looking to end up at a psychologist. But here I was, and I was grateful. A big part of me being where I was, was running away from a man. And what, now I had to run back to him? Or run to another man rather? Who was no different to him? That was my fear. Love was not the question, or a relationship. It was not to look to a man for anything. It's what my devil step-father taught me. And my father? Well... he knows where he is. Bottom line I was diagnosed with a mental breakdown and given temporary treatment. Prevention is better than cure no doubt and this was hardly a cure but it enabled me to sleep at least and to rest my mainframe. There are firewall drugs that fight for you and shield you from yourself. Chemicals to fight chemicals and triggers to fight triggers. Although I have never wanted to take any kind of medication.

At last, we succeeded with our goal—I was able to prove I had been incapacitated during my exam time. My psychologist would back me up should I encounter any resistance from the examination board. To end this long chapter—perhaps the most significant from a survivor's point of view—it would be nice to be able to say here that I was given as much time as I liked to recover and feel better before returning to any kind of taxation. That my therapist would let everybody know when I could carry on with my life. But it was just those few sessions with her and then back into the thick of it. Before the year had passed I was down to work again and pushing for that degree. I mean, since when does a little thing like a mental breakdown hold you back when so much is at stake? I was able to sit for a few exams that were scheduled towards the back end of the year. This meant that I would write most of my exams in January the following year—sitting with those that would be writing supplementary exams. There was no room for error for me. There was not going to be any second chances.

24

Holy Mischief

Room for error? Second chances? It's like a theme running through my life. And I must take every chance, and run every risk. Because it's in my nature, one, and because I enjoy it. And now and then it helps me. And it helps someone else. December 2009, my final year, back from the dead as such, back from history, making history. I had imagined my gangster habits being flushed down the drain along with everything else during my ordeal. But I somehow found myself relapsing into mischief. This time, it was not for kicks or any adrenaline. It was not for my benefit either. Call it what you like but to me, it was an act of love, a way to pay back all the goodness that was done to me by Ree. He was no commerce student but to keep his options open—and be set apart from his peers—he chose Management as his major. This came with Marketing, Operations, Strategic Management, and Corporate Finance. The first three modules were a walk in the park for him, especially Strategic Management.

He was the lecturer's pet if you ask me, the way they would engage in and outside of lectures talking about boring strategy case studies was so weird for a 22-year-old Ree. I remember how everyone would fight to have him as a member for group assignments—knowing well that they would have him to complete the entire assignment while they kept him company. It was no wonder for me to see his calling follow him years later as a Strategy Consultant. On the other hand, Corporate Finance was a thorn in the flesh for him, paradoxically and figuratively. He wrote his Corporate Finance exams four consecutive times in 2008, his final year. One exam in June and a supplementary exam in July. Another exam in December and a supplementary exam in January. Each time he would come back with 48% or 49%, so close and yet so far from the 50% passing mark. This 1% was psychologically devastating. It was about the bright future that was ahead of him and the strong likelihood of it being funnelled down the drain because of a module failure.

I could relate fully to that and found it unbearable to contemplate. There must be something I could do. That was during my second last year—his final year. The following year—my final year—we found ourselves in the same class: Corporate Finance. You can tell me later if this was mischief or not, or if it was meant to be. He swore to write the exam for the last time in June 2009, which he failed again by 1%. Even for a non-superstitious chap like him, he was convinced that he was cursed. The fact that I got 98% for the same exam only rubbed salt into the wound. Having put in his all, as I had done, he was to get nothing out. While I was to leave him behind. And all that mattered to him would be gone.

I had never seen him that shattered. He decided to drop out of school as there seemed to be no other way out for him. It broke my heart.

I remember the day like it was yesterday when he poured out his heart to me. The atmosphere was so gloomy that I didn't see the need to switch on the lights when it got dark. We sat together in silence on the bed, leaning against the wall, him staring up at the roof the whole time. I had no words to comfort him. I've never been the one to say things I didn't mean. To say to him "it's all going to be okay," not being sure about that myself, would have been a sheer insult. Especially since we were in the same class now and I had tried explaining the complex concepts to him. We would do our assignments together in the hope of getting him ready for the exam, that's the best I could do at the time. I begged him not to quit, tried quoting every African and Chinese proverb I knew about not quitting, but it didn't help.

When he stopped attending classes for a while and started looking for jobs, I knew he wasn't bluffing. I was not about to report that to his mother either. I was never a sell-out and was without a doubt not about to become one now. Loyalty was and is still everything in my world. For a long time, I wrestled with myself on how I could help him. I kept begging him to come back and give it one more try—promising to find a way out of his predicament. He agreed, eventually. I didn't have a plan then but I've always been good at thinking on my feet so I wasn't bothered about the how. I knew and trusted that at the right time the plan and opportunity to get that 50% would come knocking at my door. I was magnetic to solutions. Only this solution would include mischief, I knew that way ahead of time. I am not saying God promotes mischief but I am boldly declaring that He did orchestrate mine.

Remember my knockout, how I had dropped out, and only came back towards the back end of the exam period? With a chunk of my exams scheduled in January along with those that were writing supplementary exams? Well, here's the thing, Corporate Finance and Short-term Insurance were amongst the few modules I was able to sit for in December 2009. When I saw the list for seating arrangements I knew what I had to do. Miraculously, we were to sit in the same venue, which had never happened before in my four years at UWC (University of the Western Cape). When your surname started with an N, say, as in my case, you automatically knew who you would sit with. Anyone with a surname starting with an S like Ree would be far from us in that arrangement. I believe in omens, and boy I took that as a good omen and a confirmation from either God or the Universe. It was risky, it could have led to me being expelled, led to my dreams coming crashing down, so soon after my dark place and only returning to a possibility of seeing my light at the end of the tunnel, but I was ready to take that chance for Ree. It was the best thank you I could give him, considering all that he had done for me. Besides, when you're addicted to mischief and you get caught, trust me, there's always a way out: MORE MISCHIEF. I had been doing this for so long that repercussions didn't scare me. The word didn't exist in my vocabulary.

On the day of the exam, I asked Ree to sit parallel to my desk without telling him about my plans. When he got to the venue I realised he must have thought I meant close to me, not next to me. I quickly jumped off my seat—two desks ahead of him—and sat down again parallel to his desk. Bless him, with his background, schooling, and upbringing, my mischief was just too much for him. The thought of what was about to go down didn't cross his mind at all. He was a saint, a man of principles, good morals, and good conduct, like my other musketeer. I wonder if that was not one of the subjects they taught at their elite private schools in Cape Town?

In the exam room, each aisle had its invigilator assigned to it, located right at the back of the exam room, to get a sort of "bird's view" if you can call it that, and then there would be two invigilators at the door for an extra pair of eyes and to receive late comers without causing disruption. On top of that, there would be two chief invigilators who were responsible to hand out examinations papers, making lame announcements, and receiving our papers at the end of the session. It was maximum security. More reason to motivate me to crack it to see if I've still got it after all these years. I almost froze when they handed me my question paper, when I saw how difficult the questions were, even for "Mrs. Smarty Pants" me. I scanned through the paper, something I used to do every time I had an exam, just to calculate more or less how many marks am I aiming for.

I was never driven to get an A, nor even finish the exam paper. I saw no point in sitting for three hours sweating so you could be on the Dean's merit list. Why would I impress someone who didn't even know who I was? I was also not interested in knowing the Dean and I graduated without knowing whether it was a he or a she. I wasn't about external validation or impressing some stranger with this big title just because everyone around me was doing it. I did now and again finish the exam, just to prove a point to the so-called Dean merit list in my class. Exhibit A was the 98% in my finance exam, the second highest being less than 80%—the guy that kept the No.1 spot on the Dean's list. Also, I hated using my brain unnecessarily. I wanted to preserve it for more important things.

My musketeers called it self-sabotage but I didn't see where the sabotage was. I passed my degree in record time, my pace was working for me, I was in competition with no one but myself. Back to the exam room, I struggled to find where I could get 50% easy, that's how tough that exam was. Our lecturer must have sourced that paper from Harvard or Cambridge past exam papers—that's what they used to do when they got lazy. The terminology, concepts, the style was nothing we'd ever seen before. But I wasn't worried about myself, I knew I could always come back in January if I failed. My worry was the promise I made to Ree.

How was I going to help him when I could barely help myself? I looked harder at the questions and thought to myself *there must be a way*. I gently turned my head to the right, where Ree was seated. The look on his face was heartbreaking. He was fiddling with his calculator, sucking on the back of his pen. I sneak peeked and saw his answer book still blank, not even the word "Question 1." At that moment I decided to tear a piece of paper at the end of the question paper, using it as a scribble and workings paper I wouldn't have to hide as that was allowed during exams—it would create no suspicion at all. Talk about finding loopholes in a system! I started writing answers to the questions I was sure about, then worked my way through, taking an educated guess for the difficult questions, something I was taught during my internship (the taking an educated guess part, not the mischief). Through the educated guessing and gut feeling I started answering more questions than I had imagined—and I had faith that they would yield more than 50%. Part I of my mission was complete. I started scouting the coast for the "watchmen" using my corner eyes, then pretending to be yawning and stretching my arms when I was checking the invigilator behind me. I noticed that while their eyes were wide open, they were "slaap tigers" (sleeping tigers). I folded the piece of paper to be inconspicuous.

By this time, Ree's answer book was still relatively blank. I whispered and called him. When he looked, I handed over the inconspicuous paper which he refused to take. I could not believe it! He started reminding me how I could get expelled and never get a chance to another university. As if I didn't know that, and was taking the risk regardless! *Is he out of his mind?* I thought to myself, trying hard not to get upset. He kept shaking his head, commanding me to stop, even though his situation was hopeless. The best he could come with by the looks of things would be nothing more than 20%. If anything, he was the one who could potentially be expelled for failing Corporate Finance so many times. And here he was refusing help! I looked at the time. An hour had passed. I had to start focusing on my own answer sheet, which only had my name and student number at this stage. I started writing, so Ree could forget about what had just happened.

After finishing the last question (I always work backwards, so it was technically my first question) I checked the parameters once again. By now, invigilators get tired of standing and just watching. Truth be told, no one is built for such a long concentration span. I gently and quietly moved my chair towards my right until it was stopped by the desk legs. Then in slow motion I pushed my chair back to allow enough space for me to get up without making contact with my desk. What you must know, I am blessed with long arms. And this day, this moment, I maximized on my blessing. The movement if it was to be seen by anyone would have to be so quick they would think they had not seen it but imagined it. Cameras, if there were cameras, should not be able to track it.

Time seemed to stand still and yet in a split second I had got up and reached over and got down again with the paper now on his desk. No doubt if anyone had seen it they would have taken it for a magic trick. I was back in my seat as if I never left. Truly what he had just witnessed was the work of a magician and yet he was mad and refused to accept it. You would have thought someone had landed a crap on his desk the way he looked at the paper. It was hilarious on one hand and ridiculous on the other. His hands were shaking and he was all sweaty, out of nervousness or fear or anger, I don't know. He indicated that he was aiming at throwing the paper back at me. I told him that if he gets caught while doing it, it will look like he's the one who wrote all those answers there for me.

Now who do you think would get expelled?

"Open the damn paper" I told him "and start copying the answers. It will look like you have been doing your calculations on the side." Time was running out, like I was running out of patience. I felt like strangling him. I had thought getting him the answers was the solution, but I was contending with a man of integrity and ethics—attributes I felt were uncalled for at the time. I don't know if it was only that or if the stubbornness of a SeSotho traditional man was also at play. Or just the pride of a man, any man, not wanting to accept help. I was working with two mantras at the time: "desperate times calls for desperate measures" and "anything is possible, just never take your eyes off the goal". I used the desperation mantra to remind him what was at stake here. And I think it appealed to his ethical sense to think that there was at least a mantra that covered it. We don't always want to do the things we do but sometimes we have to do them. He eventually gave way, leaving me with less than an hour and a half to focus on my work—not much time for such a difficult exam.

After the session he was not a happy man, not by a long shot. My hour and a half became a lecture and a half as he told me how I should start taking my life seriously, how much potential I have, a bright future ahead of me blah blah blah. It all came in one ear and went out the other without touching sides.

My partner-in-mischief musketeer on the other hand celebrated my "bravery" by doffing her hat to me and shaking my hand for what I had done. She was totally impressed—the reaction I had been looking for from Ree. Her surname started with a K and we normally would have been assigned to the same venue, but not this time. She was like: "Bra, I wish I was there. Would gladly have taken that paper off Ree's hands." She always spoke my language, she was a PK (pastor's kid) but that didn't seem to matter to either of us. I embraced both her sides—the church side and the real her. I didn't know and didn't care about the cause or drive behind her mischief, I was only happy to have a partner in crime.

I don't mind calling it holy mischief, it was not for my junkie habit or my adrenaline rush, not for myself at all, but for someone else.

It was about showing my gratitude to the one soul who was there for me even when he didn't have to be, the one soul who never gave up on me when I had no one to get me out of my deep, dark pit of depression that led to my mental breakdown. Unfortunately the only way I could thank him was the best way I knew how. I've given him so many gifts but to date I'm happiest with this one. Priceless I'm thinking, but I know he would disagree. Fast forward, results came out, between us 51% and 54%. You can say I took from my marks and gave them to him so we could both pass. Almost half the class failed and had to come back in January for supplementary exams. Over time, I gradually eased off on the mischief as it scared the hell out of Ree. It didn't exactly help me that the career path I chose revolved around Ethics and Integrity. It was a huge adjustment for me, introducing me to a version of myself I never thought was possible. It felt so abnormal and totally uncomfortable for me to choose between the path that seemed like the only way to govern my life and ethics that were founded on moral principles. Of course now and again it does pop up out of nowhere.

Like when I briefly stayed with my aunts and cousins upon my arrival in Cape Town. We were about 11 altogether under one roof, myself included. Imagine a weekly load of laundry for 11 people, hand washed! On Saturday mornings they would take out the laundry and put it on this beautiful well-watered lawn, fill the black garbage drums with water, and begin to put the clothes and soap in. My older aunt would begin with "I need to make a quick call, there's no signal in this yard" and leave, "looking" for a better location for the "signal." My cousin would be next with a "smoke break" that required going to look for her smoking friends. My younger aunt would finish off with "going to the shop" around the corner—"I'll be back in a minute" she said. Leaving me with the mountain all to myself. 30 minutes would go by, none of them were back, an hour later, no sign of them. I was taken aback but not bothered. Was this a conspiracy of some kind? Meanwhile I would wash my clothes and my grandpa's (Daphney's brother), rinse them nicely and hang them. I'd have done the same for them if they were there, helping me. But I'd take their clothes as they were from the water—full of powder soap—and hang them like that on the washing line. Then I'd spill the water out on the grass and let the drums dry out. They'd be back in the afternoon by the time they estimated I'd be done with the laundry and the garden tidied up—no apologies or explanations. When the laundry would get dry my older aunt would ask my cousin to take it off the washing line and pack it away. After work on week days they'd have their tops off and be walking around the house in their bras, scratching their bodies off, complaining about bug bites, how much the bug bites had ruined their day. From where I was standing their bodies seemed to glow in the dark like traffic lights, constantly red. I would enjoy it all in silence, watching them scratching their thighs uncontrollably too, scratching everywhere. It was only after some months that they caught on, I wasn't washing their dirty clothes, and what they thought was bugs was actually powder soap. Here's the funny thing, they had nothing to say, explicitly or implicitly. They asked me nothing and could ask me nothing. Here's my thing, how do you begin confronting me about being malicious when you know you were being malicious yourself? Not only malicious but cruel. If there was to be a conversation about it would it not need be about how dumb you were to think such cheap tactics would work on someone from my hood, on my level of operating? I was always street smart and quickly picked up on their game from day one. I sniffed it from a distance, don't ask me how, it came naturally. The only way to deal with such evil was holy mischief— to save myself from being a victim again of domestic abuse—abuse so clearly prevalent in our communities where staying with relatives is concerned. From there I was banned from washing the clothes— including my own! From then on my duty would be to take them off the washing line. I was happy enough to be demoted thus and happier still to be in a position where I could check to see if my clothes were being washed properly or not.

What I had done back then seemed like a simple solution to my problem until I came across a client of mine recently. She told me that she dropped out of school, ran away from home and lived in the streets in a nearby town because her aunt would demand that she hand wash their laundry on a weekly basis—without any help from her cousins or the aunt herself. There were seven of them in that family and I remember how triggered she was, like she was reliving the moments of blood oozing from wrists rubbed raw from the prolonged friction of hand washing with powder soap. You can imagine how unbearable it was for her to choose the streets over home. To think she was under the age of 12 at the time and had nowhere to go. To think this devilishness shattered her future—robbed her of whatever opportunity education could have given her. Don't get me wrong now, it was brutal abuse, I'm not taking away from her pain and suffering, my experience could have easily have been hers, only my holy mischief saved me from the victim mode and took me to solution mode. I had already passed through too much violation than to let my aunts think they had what it takes to break my spirit. I was not so easily breakable. *Holy Mischief, you will always have a special place in my heart. I have so much respect for you. I have seen you getting me out of dangerous situations, you have gone as far as saving my best friend's marriage doing what you do best. Letting you go was one of the hardest things I ever had to do. You were my first love, my companion, my best friend and my protector. May you keep on protecting every little girl that feels alone out there until such a time your duties are no longer needed.*

VI

Part Six

"Never be afraid to trust an unknown future to a known God." -Corrie Ten Boom

25

Dear God

They say the word affliction pronounced: /əˈflɪkʃ(ə)n/ is synonymous with suffering, distress, pain, trouble, misery, hardship, disorder, indisposition, disease, illness, malady and ailment. I just saw it fit to acknowledge and thank you for always being there when I was going through hell and for making it back. I have always wondered how come I managed to keep my sanity through it all, even when it felt like I was losing my mind. I still make silly mistakes. I feel like I'm far from being the version you had in mind when you created me. I'm no saint, I still sin so many times even though I know better. My spirit is willing but my flesh is weak. It's just that sin is naturally hard to resist for me especially my temper but I trust you to finish the good work you have begun in me—I can't conquer it on my own. I need your grace.

You must have had me in mind when you made your mercies to be new everyday. I can't help but believe that I wouldn't be as wiser to recognize where I'm falling short if it was not for your affliction. Perhaps I wouldn't be as kind if it was not for all those life-changing afflictions that brought me to my knees—where no amount of money could buy off my suffering. I've always suspected that maybe, just maybe, the pain that I went through was the best possible way for you to prepare me for what lies ahead of me. Even your word says something like narrow is the road that leads to life and few there be that find it.

I remember always asking you if you can't find any other way to train my hands for war and prepare my fingers for battle but now I realize my breakthrough never lay in running away from my Goliaths and Herods and Pharaohs of this earth, but to get to a place of accepting my affliction for what it is:

Training to make me your hammer and weapon of war,

Teaching to use me to crush nations and kingdoms,

Coaching to shatter horses and riders,

Tutoring to shatter chariots and their drivers.

I wouldn't have known about my giant-killing anointing that you have placed down inside me—which needed to be activated by facing giants. For me, this meant making peace with everything that's happened to me and trusting that it was not a stumbling block but a stepping stone for where I needed to go. I hate admitting this but I needed to be broke like hell—so I could learn to budget with my money, not with my words—before you, Father could bless me exceedingly and abundantly beyond what I can ever imagine or ask for.

In retrospect, there was no other way to swim with sharks and overpower arrogant pricks with my presence.

Pardon my ungodly language, it's one of the sins I am working on that I just told you about. It made no sense for me not to say it out loud since you know my thoughts before I think them, and you examine my heart and know everything about me. You know what I'm going to say even before I say it. What is the point of hiding my nakedness from you? Who am I fooling? Since you cannot be mocked.

As I was saying, I'm grateful for all the pain. From the pain, I was able to develop resilience that no devil monger can take away from me now—even if he tried. I have a confession to make though. If I were to choose to go through pain voluntarily, I'd be like "no, thank you, I'm good." But, and this is a big BUT.

If I were to be shown the result of your beautiful work Father—that would turn me into the version of myself I am today—my response would certainly be different. I wouldn't take the affliction on willingly, of course, only thee John Wick would raise his hand. I know you're omniscient but I'm still not sure if you know him. That's because I'm not sure if you watch TV. You don't strike me as the type, even though you're omnipresent. Just picture a modernized and sophisticated version of Chuck Norris. So as tempting as the outcome would have been, I would have probably required a push in the right direction. The first step to help me accept what happened to me was looking at where I am right now. I may not necessarily be where I wanted to be but I want to believe that I am not where I used to be. I am where you, Lord, want me to be.

The Bible and science agree that gold has to go through fire to be refined. Being a miner myself I remember how personally I took it when I witnessed the process of refining minerals as if the extraction from the ores was not gut-wrenching enough. It was no longer a business decision but the best decision for the mineral to reach its optimum purity—a premium product that inherently translated to premium pricing—even though that was not the point at all. I feel like it's the same way with you Father. You don't refine us through the fire so we can be these gold trophies but rather to make a premium version of us—a version we wouldn't have known existed—a version that is a reflection of your eminence, magnificence, and majesty on earth.

How comforting it is to look myself in the mirror and see a stone that was rejected by builders becoming the chief cornerstone. As the Lord's doing. How marvellous in my eyes? It is with sincere gratitude and great admiration that I get to dedicate my book in remembrance of your legacy—not the blasphemy around me that has corrupted what has always been pure and holy.

Thank you for making me in your image—so fearfully and wonderfully complex. Thank you for giving me a story for my glory. I love you.

26

The ultimate cost of unsubscribing

Y ou might be surprised here or you might not but in the middle of the year 2010—four years after leaving the place where everything I had been taught about Him only repulsed me—I came to a new understanding of Christ that enabled me to surrender my life to Him and accept Him as Lord and Saviour. There was no pressure now to conform or uphold the family name. Neither was there any incentive or agenda or ulterior motive. Accepting Jesus as my Lord was no masquerade for me. It was not about mere utterance while acquiring the licence to do evil in the name of God. I still step out of line, yes, I sin more often than I should—still have my flesh popping up when provoked—but I don't hide behind the name of the Lord as the hypocrites do, but trust rather in that name to help me to become a vessel worthy of being called by that name. I see myself as He sees me, define myself as He defines me: a masterpiece and a work-in-progress at the same time. And it didn't take a dramatic encounter—or a conversion along my way to Damascus—or to be blinded by glory—for me to consider a relationship with Jesus. You'll have to laugh when you think it was on a Sunday morning again and with me attending church—but for none of those other stupid reasons from before. This Sunday was different. I was outside, going on with my normal routine when I heard this beautiful worship from a distance. It was like nothing I've heard before. I asked Ree's aunt if she knew where the sound was coming from and she told me. I'm not sure what it was about that music. Me I was no nightingale. Neither did I have much to sing about growing up.

But the music picked me up—almost like a pied piper tune—and there I was, attending church again. I can't recall anything about the sermon or what Pastor Shwane from RUCC Ministries (Cape Town) was going on about but no doubt there was a reason I was there and something was happening all around me and inside me. The usual altar call afterwards that I gladly ignored. Needed Jesus? Me? I had needed Him back then, no doubt. Now? I could take care of myself. People were going up and he was ready to pray. But he said there was someone in the audience that "has a divine appointment with Jesus but is hesitating to come to the front." I recall sitting there annoyed at this person for delaying the church service because I was hungry and wanted to go home. I sat there scouting for someone who looked like they had a big decision to make but to my disappointment I didn't find anyone.

Pastor Shwane kept singing softly with a smile and said he's patiently waiting on that one soul—which he was already thanking God for. I wanted to punch him in the face for what I deemed as arrogance. I was ready to grab my bag and go home. *There's always the next Sunday for this* I thought in my mind— you can't hold us ransom over one indecisive and confused soul. I stood up with my bucket hand bag, left my seat and worked my way across toward the end of the row where I was sitting, heading for the aisle. As I got to the aisle, instead of turning left towards the exit, I turned right towards the altar. I wished for the floors to open up and swallow me alive. And as I was about to turn back again a voice says to me: "they're waiting for you." I've put it down that way because it was not a voice in my mind like the others but a voice as clearly spoken as any voice would be—only inside of me. You can't refuse a voice like that. I proceeded as directed, toward the altar, and I wonder if it was the first time ever I was directed and I willingly obeyed—but with caution, verifying in my head if that is what I truly wanted. I continued walking—against everything I had raised myself to be—like an obedient puppy, tail between my legs. I couldn't know, couldn't be sure if what I was about to do was the best thing for me. I got there and the pastor asked the church to applaud me—what I had done was apparently a bold move. Not so, I was thinking. More like an inner force compelling me—leading me on regardless. I can't say much more than this, only, due to my childhood experience with church, I vowed not to take a church membership but be a regular visitor instead. I kept my vow, then broke it at some point, but went back on keeping it till today. Once bitten, twice shy. But to put the experience into my own words—without comparing divinity to humanity—or reducing it to the scale of humanity—I can say falling in love with Jesus was like falling in love with Ree.

I can't tell you at what point I got so deep and was way over heels. What I can tell you for sure is: I dated Jesus for a good two years with no pressure of committing for the rest of my life. I must say though, we didn't have the time—nor the appetite—for flirting. Again, exactly how things turned out between Ree and I. I wonder if it is not that pressure—the lack of it—that made my relationship with Jesus what it is today: perfectly personal. It's not based on the opinions and standards of others—it's about how He wants me to connect and be intimate with Him. What's working between Him and someone else may not necessarily work with me.

I can't help but wonder if Christian spirituality is not about that after all? Perhaps it would explain why God said to Joshua He will be with him as He was with Moses. He didn't say "I will do with you what I did with Moses". The outcome remains the same, but the methods are intricately personal and customized. Sure the Israelites had to cross the Jordan River with brother Joshua just like they had to cross the Red Sea. But what they didn't know is, it didn't have to be the same way Moses led them through the Red Sea. Joshua's victory in crossing the Jordan River had to be peculiar and specific to Joshua in a way that was unique to him and God. That's what makes any relationship special. I was deliberate in my approach and took my spiritual journey one day at a time.

My four years at university were enough to reverse the brainwash, the church trauma, and my hatred for God. I was an adult now, ready to exercise the faculties of my curiosity and give God a chance to prove to me that He is not this cruel scary man with a big long beard that is out to get us every time we sin—even though He does discipline us out of love when we do sin. He's not waiting on the sidelines like a hard taskmaster to strike us with lightning bolts whenever we don't see eye to eye with Him. I look at my relationship with Jesus from how it started to how it is now and I look at my relationship with Ree and can't help but notice the similarity. It's like my marriage is a shadow of my relationship with Jesus. I began inviting Ree to church now and again—me being an introvert, there were times I felt out of place and could do with some company. I had no intention of converting him into anything he wasn't—something he had no point of reference with. He grew up in a Methodist church, that was all he'd ever known. To reach common ground we would alternate and go to *my* church every second Sunday and if we had five Sundays in a month he would come my way. It was an arrangement that worked out so well for both of us.

I recall one service when after church they called for single women to stand on one side and married ones on the other. I was on the fence! Ree and I were not married then but I was far from being single. I wasn't about to pull Simon Peter's stunt on Ree and pretend like I had never seen him before just so I could blend in with church and avoid judgment. Of course they discouraged dating and *vat en sit* (shacking up) but I wasn't about to let anything compromise what I had with either Ree or God. Yes, there was an option of introducing Ree as my cousin at church as I've seen so many people doing, but who was fooling who? God cannot be mocked. I feared God more than I feared men. And imagine having to look over my shoulders at the shopping mall when strolling with my boyfriend—crossing fingers and toes not to bump into church folks? That was a full-time job I was just not ready for.

Growing up in the midst of hypocrites had vaccinated me against hypocrisy. When all else fails, go public. I nudged the pastor and his wife, Zan introduce me rather, I said, and my predicament—not so they could approve but so I could sleep easy knowing I was walking in the light and not living a lie. With money saved up and a move to the suburbs we saw a change of churches—though we still kept in touch with them as our first pastors and visited when we could. Churches are churches all over, all have their strengths and weaknesses. While in one I had come to a crossroads with Jesus, here I would find a fork. And I would have to decide quickly. Imagine how long it's taken just to share this with you. But they wanted me to share it all in a matter of minutes. In the name of "deliverance" they were wanting us to deliver information to them about our past. This kind of digging meant revealing a past I was not ready to talk about—not to strangers anyway. They told me that what had happened to me as a child signified that I was very special—that I was a Joseph of my family. I must have been seriously screwed up because I believed them. I suddenly felt guilty for distancing myself and starting a new life—one with freedom and peace. They say regret is stronger than gratitude, I think they're right. Suddenly I was filled with so much regret—I regretted listening to my psychologist about cutting ties with my so-called family—even though Elizabeth and I never stopped talking on the phone. Suddenly perspective shifted, I spoke to Ree and we used some of our savings to renovate and extend Elizabeth's house. I started buying her and my siblings clothes from the city—a status symbol in our home town. Suddenly I wanted to make her proud. I wanted to put the family name on a map. I guess it's easier to replace forgiveness with "it's all in the past." I say that because deep down I knew I had not forgiven Elizabeth but it was more comfortable to carry on like nothing happened instead of addressing issues. The fact that she was able to secretly attend my little sister's graduation over a one week short course in the Free State but refused to attend my graduation ceremony in Cape Town made me assume that she was not happy that I graduated—like she was secretly hoping that I would flunk and give up. It was a norm in Tarkastad, remember? What she didn't know was, I was no statistic. I was a different breed, somehow. I was not upset that she didn't come, I was upset by her reasons. I had specifically told her that her monstrous husband was not allowed anywhere near the university gates—let alone my graduation ceremony. She told me she wouldn't be able to come without him because *people from church and the community* will put one and one together and know that there was trouble in paradise. She was not ready to answer their valid questions. This was the cost of unsubscribing that I had to pay.

I thought stepping on uncharted territory with no plan was the cost—I learned the hard way that that was just the beginning. I was now feeling indebted to her for all those calls—checking up on me after I had left home with swollen lips and bruised ribs in June 2007. While I was grateful that she had not abandoned me on one hand, on the other hand I hated her for everything that she did to me as an accomplice. Truth be told, she abandoned me from as early as a toddler borderline preschooler. It's called emotional abandonment. The same way that she financially abandoned me at university to fend for myself. But somehow I was desperate to silence those feelings and didn't want to face my demons.

Elizabeth was one of the demons I battled to look in the eye. It's like somehow I was scared not to belong. Well, that's how it seemed for a long time. But quite frankly it was the fear of solitude that kept me up at night. I was scared of making it official—that I was on my own. I was scared of facing my past and every ugly detail about it. What no one told me was the beauty of solitude. There's something powerful and magical about meeting yourself within yourself. No busyness, no friends, no functions, no church, just you with yourself. You get to learn about yourself, your nicely dressed wounds, and you get to reinvent yourself. Two years after my graduation Ree and I decided to get married. Again for the same reasons she gave me on my grad, my mother did not come to my wedding. She gave me an ultimatum, "it's either I come with *your* father or I don't come at all—people in this town talk, you know that." I was left with an egg on my face as everyone wanted to know where my mother was? At this stage, they knew that I was fatherless. It was this event that made me revisit my Christian walk. I had been duped and taught the wrong way of forgiveness. It suddenly dawned on me that for the church counsellors to compare me with Joseph in the Bible was a sheer insult to what I had to endure from a young age. For those of you that last heard about him in Sunday School, let me refresh your memories:

- One, he was his father's favourite child and got preferential treatment—which explains the multi-coloured Gucci robe. On the other hand, I was the unfavoured child.
- Two, Joseph was temporarily thrown in an empty pit with no water, (Genesis 37:24). I don't mean to take away from the ordeal of being all alone down there, hungry, thirsty and possibly scared to death but compare that to packing bricks with flames of fire

using my bare hands for so many years.

- Three, he was 17 years of age when he was sold into slavery. I was only 6 years old under that train and 11 when I started with child slavery. I haven't mentioned the torture that came with being constantly assaulted as a young girl by a man who called himself my father.

I could carry on but I'm sure you get the picture now. From this place I started defining forgiveness in my own terms and what it meant to me, not to brother Joseph—the same way that Joseph defined his own forgiveness and explicitly showed favouritism towards his little brother, Benjamin, serving him five times more food and drink than his brothers when they gathered for dinner (Genesis 43:34). This meant being okay with detaching myself from my mother without feeling guilty and being able to ignore harmful projections like "but she's your mother" from people who are often misinformed about trauma—and about having the one person who was meant to nurture you being the one to sell you out and become your primary abuser.

I say primary abuser because it was only when I looked back at my life at the age of 30—pondering on Elizabeth's confusing behaviour—that I started asking myself a question that must have been from the wise 11-year-old me. *What if Mama was behind all this abuse, but had the perfect candidate to execute the brutality that couldn't be possibly associated with a social worker?* My inquisitive mind didn't end there, a follow up question came. *What if her husband just happened to be a foolish bully that she could easily manipulate to do the dirty work for her?* I remember the shock I had to my own thoughts—I can't describe my physical reaction to that discovery—I just knew that was not what I wanted to hear, not after believing that my step-father had robbed me of the first 16 years of my life. I didn't want to go there, but I did, I traced back my steps—including when I was falsely accused. It was a set up!

My own mother had set me up and witnessed my flesh being ripped out by a belt buckle—the same way she set me up and watched my womb being hammered by the table—the same way she was quick to report Rhoda's suspicions of abuse. As I battled to swallow the pill—the truth about my devilish angel—she made my job easier for me.

Fast forward to a few years later which is a story for another day. I'm at home with you-know-who when my step-brother dies—yes, him. He had changed his ways by now but I guess he had to pay for his sins nonetheless—allegedly stabbed over his long-time girlfriend. I'm taller than Elizabeth, she's short—it's to do with a father—mine. Funny how genes play a part here to reveal to me the truth. As if someone somewhere wanted me to know something. And maybe this leads us on to what will come next when we begin the next story. How I was even in that house again to begin with. Because of her height she asked me to get two of her insurance policies on top of her wardrobe. Because of my height I handed them over. Then she asked me to contact the two insurance companies on her behalf.

Call it what you will, fate or autopilot or divine intervention, I don't know. Looking for the phone numbers I couldn't help but notice that my name was not listed as a beneficiary in either of the policies. The beneficiaries were of course her husband, my two siblings, my step-brother, and a few distant relatives. But here's the strange thing—in the moment my mind didn't put two and two together. My eyes saw my name wasn't there but my brain didn't question that. My faculties failed to register somehow. Or maybe for some higher purpose the information was withheld from me. Who knows what was happening behind the scenes but Elizabeth on autopilot was an on and off thing, come and go. The following day she called me to explain why my name wasn't there. I brushed her off as if it did not matter to me but in fact my mind hadn't processed what I had just discovered. It wasn't denial—if I could name it—but a delayed reaction, God knows. It was only three months later—in a random conversation with an old lady—that my world was momentarily shattered. In talking with her about a mother and her daughter with no father and her life cover policy for her daughter my light bulb flashed. I did not exist in my mother's world! I was not included in any of her funeral covers and life insurance policies! I was not included in her life! I know it's strange but that's exactly how it happened. I'm reminded here of Elijah on the mountain top surrounded by the elements—how God was not in the storm, not in the whirlwind, not in the thunder and lightning, but the still small voice. I had to silence the noise around me and listen to the voice within me—that is the voice that always knows what is best for me. I had to stop forming my definition of forgiveness and how to act on it based on the opinions of those who didn't have to live with the consequences—the cost of unsubscribing. I fought too hard and too long for my freedom for me to find myself a prisoner of people's opinions. I didn't know how to move on, but I also knew that I did not want to go back to that emotional place. Sometimes, when we feel stuck, the most logical step to take is not to go back—and that's not the same as standing still. It takes bravery to walk away, no doubt, but it takes courage not to go back to what you know did not serve you.

The question for me was: to cut or not to cut the umbilical cord with Mama? Life was hard for me. I was confused and conflicted. I didn't know whether to turn left or turn right.

Questions, questions… How did I get here? How does one get to a point of being ostracized by family without doing them any wrong? What would I say to my children when they ask my help to complete a family tree at school? It was like I was not in alignment. What I thought, felt, said and actioned was totally misaligned. Have you ever been so violated by someone that you were conflicted—what you felt about them inside was totally a mismatch to how you treated them?

Somehow your actions would be so polite—in the name of avoiding drama—feeling compelled to hold diplomatic conversations just so you don't come across as funny—but your mind wants to rip their heart out for what they'd done to you? I was ready to cut all ties and burn my umbilical cord but if that was good for me why did I now feel bad? Why did it feel so wrong? Here I was, caught between two worlds. Suddenly, cutting her off didn't seem to be as simple as I had rehearsed in my head. This showed me how complex the human mind is, how complex I was. There is the head of course, and the heart, and they can be two different worlds you live in. The one processes information and makes decisions but the other just feels and continues to get hurt. After sitting down and doing an audit—noting every good thing Elizabeth had done for me against the bad—only one page of the journal was good and the rest bad. One thing that I was grateful for—what I used to blackmail myself—was no matter what conception, she chose to keep me. She didn't have to but she did, I could say. That's what I told myself when I wanted to justify my feelings for her. But then I couldn't reconcile the relentless consistency of her actions against me. Could she be regretting keeping me? I couldn't help but wonder. And I wonder if this does not have something to do with the ultimate cost of unsubscribing.

Why did she not abort me at once if she still wanted to keep her man? The record played over and over. Back street abortions were no doubt available back then. *Perhaps it was not so easy back then for rural girls.* That's another thought that came to mind. It was against the law. The 1975 Abortion and Sterilization Act (ASA) required a doctor's permission and sometimes a magistrate's clearance—something she would not have got. It was only later—six years after I was born—that they replaced the act with the Choice on Termination of Pregnancy Act—giving women free access to abortion services early on in the pregnancy. Talk about the Lord working in mysterious ways! The invisible hand that hid and protected me from being aborted! It makes me think of Moses when he was floated in a basket and left to the river by his mother. I want to believe that his mother knew that Pharaoh's daughter when she would come to bathe there would have compassion on him. This would explain why she posted Miriam nearby—Moses' sister—to watch when this would happen. It was a risk, no doubt, but a calculated risk. She was ready to relinquish the child and let go—the ultimate cost of unsubscribing. It was not a beach in Camps Bay but the Nile—home of Nile crocodiles. Anything could have happened there along the bank, hidden among the reeds.

Choices!

She knew it would cost her dearly to disobey the King's orders and unsubscribe. But she also knew that it would cost her even more to give her son away for execution.

Choice 1: "Have my baby executed by Pharaoh."

Choice 2: "Have crocodiles eat my baby."

Of course with the first choice, there was no chance of survival. The probability was 0. There was no two ways about it, no negotiations. But with the basket the chances might be in his favour. She gave her son a chance to live—and a good life it turned out to be. Isn't that what mothers do when they know they can't have you? Don't they set you up for a chance to fight? A chance to live a normal life that they cannot provide? Wouldn't that be a win-win situation? I couldn't help but wonder if the invisible hand that protected Moses and later drew him out from the water was not the same invisible hand that protected me throughout my childhood and pulled me out of that moving train. With a secretive mother like mine you can't help but imagine all possibilities. I had some tough choices to make, and unfortunately, the answers I was looking for were not forthcoming. I had to make my choices based on vibes—and vibes don't lie. The first step for me was defining the meaning of family and what it meant for me. I realized that I was too important to waste my time and energy on people who did not deserve me to begin with. By now, I knew my worth and could not settle for anything less than appreciation and belonging. I wasn't going to settle for being tolerated for what I could bring to the table. I had to draw a line.

My relationship with my mother was way too expensive, it was costing me my peace. I always tell my clients in the fast-paced world we live in, it's all too easy to get caught up in the whirlwind of responsibilities and lose sight of what truly matters. Amidst the chaos of life, we must learn to prioritize and preserve our inner peace. Keeping inner peace is an essential aspect of maintaining our overall well-being. The ability to stay centered and grounded under any circumstances allows us to navigate challenges with grace and discernment. In addition, a calm mind can enhance creativity, improve relationships, and promote effective problem solving. One way to maintain our inner peace is by setting clear boundaries.

Establishing healthy limits between ourselves and others can prevent us from being overwhelmed by external demands. Respecting our values helps us avoid situations that may cause distress or harm our mental health. Boundaries are not just about saying no; they also involve prioritizing self-care and self-respect. Dedicating time for activities that nourish the body and mind can strengthen our emotional resources. In doing so, we allow ourselves to be more present for the people who matter most.

Drawing boundaries can be difficult for many, as the fear of disappointing others can overpower the need to prioritize our well-being. However, standing firmly by our decisions and communicating them assertively enhances self-esteem and helps develop a stronger sense of identity. Another critical aspect of maintaining inner peace is not compromising on love—both for ourselves and others. Compromising on love means settling for less than what we deserve or need in a relationship. It often leaves us feeling depleted and frustrated, which ultimately hinders our ability to cultivate true happiness. When we do not compromise on love, we nurture relationships that uplift us and enrich our lives. We should choose those who value our worth just as much as they value their own:

- They should provide support and encouragement during times of growth and challenge.
- They should engage in open and honest communication while holding space for constructive dialogue.

In turn, we must also cultivate the same qualities within ourselves, as love is a reciprocal process that enriches both parties involved. In essence, preserving our inner peace relies on putting in consistent effort to maintain balance and wellness in our lives. Drawing boundaries and not compromising on love are essential aspects of nurturing a tranquil spirit.

By prioritizing self-care and cultivating relationships with those who appreciate our true value, we can find serenity even in the most turbulent of times. I started learning that it's OK to belong to yourself, by yourself, until you get people that will meet you where you are, for who you are, with unconditional love and appreciation. That is my definition of family. With that being said, as much as I feel sorry for the wounded little Elizabeth, I still have unfinished business with my mother.

27

Glorious victory

Next up, my internship. Now I was done with exams, mental health slightly improved and stabilized a little, I had to answer for absconding for as long as I did and going beyond my approved study leave. I had to answer also for the missed calls I deliberately ignored—calls I had no clue how to handle in the situation. Part of me was also embarrassed and ashamed of what had just happened—embarrassed that a professional like me had dropped the ball, let the side down, not lived up to expectations. I saw it as something wrong with me and I didn't want anything to be wrong with me. Of course, I was in denial but that didn't stop me still from wanting to be perfect and wanting to be the best at anything there was to do.

I was ashamed of myself—not because I had let anybody down, but because I had let myself down. That's something else I haven't mentioned. That thing of being recognized and being appreciated and being acknowledged for who you are. For having achieved something at least. Like coming first in class or being first in your school or completing Matric but nobody celebrates with you, nobody throws you a party, no one says anything at all.

Through life it was always me on my own and no one ever acknowledging me for anything, but rather the opposite. Treating me like I had achieved nothing at all and never would. And that really was their wish for me, never to achieve anything at all, and always to fail. And stay exactly where I was. Where I was under them and their control. So I had resorted to not trying to meet anybody's standards, or looking for any approval, but to meet my own standards, and secure my own approval. And here I was not having met them nor being approved by them. That's how it goes when you hit the wall at last on your own expectations.

By now I had quit my job at the Writing Center, I had only my retail job to keep me going. Now, if ever, was a time for mothers, but really… if by now I had managed, I would continue to manage. Sure enough she had sent me a little thing here and there and I remember it because it was so rare, so few and far between. It seemed to mean a lot more to me because of that. Just because it was coming from her. Was this love? But no, love is always there, always in support, always concerned. Always able to find a way. And maybe that is what at last drove me back to myself and my original plan. See this through and face whatever comes with it. And I appreciate that to this day, the courage I found to go back, to face the music, pick up the pieces— mental breakdowns notwithstanding. At this point I may pass you on as I was passed on from one life support system to the other. I have had a man in my life that supported me, who supports me now, here is another. I have had role models, mentors, here is another. Of course I had to report to the CEO first and it did not go well. Not in the beginning, anyway. He delivered his verbal warning but revoked it by the time I left his office. That had something to do with Khulekani, one of the co-founders. He was a giant of a man in more ways than one—no less than six and a half feet tall, bald, pitch black with a strong American accent. And scary too—although he believes up to now he is good looking. He was one of the directors that happened to see something in me from the beginning and kept on cultivating it. I'd have avoided him at all costs if it was not for his playful character and ear-to-ear smile in tense meetings. He took me under his wing and like Funeka he never formalized the mentorship. "Truth is found in action" says my 11 year old daughter—I don't know how she knows. He was just like that. His actions spoke louder than words. He was (still is) not a person of many words—except when he was telling a story. And with the story, no doubt, or any other thing, came a cigarette. Given that I came out of that internship without lung cancer—God forbid—I don't see any chances of me and lung-cancer becoming an item in the future. He would invite me to tag along every time he went on a smoke break—several times a day. On entering his glass office I'd find his hand flicking the spent ashes into a round silver ashtray. He would push back from the desk while pickpocketing for a lighter—that was already in his hand—then drape a black trench coat over his shoulders and make his way out with me to the balcony. In the mornings he would open a sealed cigarette packet, in the afternoons he would open another, tossing the other away.

"Khulz do you ever read the notice on those packs?" I would ask with curiosity. "Smoking kills!" He would look me sideways with white eyes in a black face. "Shut up." His giggle afterwards implied he had no valid reason for his addiction or had no solid defence for a counterargument. He had two things in common with Funeka: they both took their own sweet time to study the opponent in the boardroom—seemingly outwitting them—especially the arrogant ones. From there, with good manners, with humility, with a deadly combination of EQ and IQ, they would proceed to eliminate and destroy whatever well-crafted argument. Secondly, they were silent assassins. They were never loud, never vocal, never quick to talk, but quick to listen rather. "Be more ready to hear" says Solomon. Better to be taken for a wise man for not opening your mouth than show you are a fool by opening it. Among the wise and prudent they taught me the loudest person in the room is the weakest. In light of that I would warn anyone: beware of the quiet one. It's not the dog that barks that you need to be wary of. And what is it the say about empty vessels making the most noise?

It was about a decade or so later that I learned that Funeka was actually groomed by Khulekani. I take this as a double blessing, a double anointing, that I feel doubly responsible for. They wouldn't have imparted such greatness to me for me to keep it to myself.

On my first day back at work he called me to his office. As per our routine, it ended up on the balcony. He drew deeply from his cigarette before turning to me. "Where the hell have you been?" he said, exhaling. I pretended to be drowning in smoke, waving away the clouds. How to answer him truthfully, with integrity, without embarrassment and shame? He sure as hell was going to see through anything less. I settled on a condensed version of the truth, to do with my past, rather than what had just happened. I couldn't take the risk of being perceived as an imbalanced emotional wreck that couldn't handle the heat. "So, what are you planning to do with your overdue deadlines?" he said—giving me an opening to negotiate. I took my chances and asked for an extension. He laughed me off with a smile. "No, I want my research. This is the real world Missy." Nevertheless there was that side to him that was human, that would listen. Maybe my story was something he could appreciate. And maybe that was what the routine was about—stepping out from the corporate world for a while to enjoy a fresh breath of sanity. Even if it was clouded with tobacco smoke. He took his own time then to share with me a bit about his past. How he struggled also, and how he overcame. I shouldn't let my personal life affect my work, he said.

"You see all these people behind us?"—pointing back to the open plan area of equity analysts and dealers. "Do you think they don't have personal battles to contend with?" So I was no different to anyone else? My problems were no bigger than anyone else's problems? How could anyone know, who had not lived my life? It seemed impossible that they could all have been like mine. I'm no spoiled brat. He seemed to see into my eyes that I was disappointed. Perhaps he saw reason there to say something else later. But he did give me for the time being an indirect script on how to make sure I wasn't fired by the CEO.

In retrospect, that advice moulded me for what was a rough yet rewarding road ahead of me. But at the time it was his intervention, more than anything, that put me back on track with my career.

Soon I was back in my groove being trusted with more meaningful responsibilities—requiring less supervision. As the head of research he honed my skills as a researcher to that level where I can say today I have not stepped into those shoes for nothing. He also taught me how immaterial your research can be if you lack the skill to package it and deliver it effectively to your audience. Here was my bread and butter, my lamb chop, my milk and honey, my speciality—not only what I could be good at but what I could excel at—what fired all my faculties and brought my potential into white hot focus. Truly it was my bread and butter but also it was my oxygen—I lived and breathed what I was doing then—and I live and breathe it now.

I never stopped communicating with my mentors when my internship came to an end. I had adopted them as my tribe—that's if they didn't adopt me first. But six months later I was still walking the streets, walking my heels off. Graduate or not, great intern or not, no job. Then a window opening, or a door, I don't know. Perhaps a stairway to heaven. But it required a minimum of 5 years related professional working experience and I had only that six months. But I was well aware and prepared for what I was up against. It was my internship that had prepared me for this moment. Not at one stage did I feel out of my element. I was not bothered by being underqualified. I applied with the faith that I would bag the role regardless. Upon signing my employment contract, the HR consultant said to me: "whoever your mentor is, keep him. He's the reason we hired you." Needless to say I had made Khulekani my reference. And he never told me when they called him. He did what he did in secret, not seeking any glory or favours.

I still have his note I keep in my mental archives, a short email he sent me, congratulating me. *Keep that light in your eyes shining Little Miss. It will take you far. There is greatness upon you. Khulz.* No doubt he's another one-of-a-kind and it was then that I started to wonder if the light he was talking about was not shining too bright for those who wanted to kill it—not knowing that killing my light wouldn't make theirs shine any brighter. Not that you can bury greatness either, mind you. Who is great enough to overthrow greatness anyway? Other than the one entrusted with that greatness? Having had my fair share of traumas that have inherently shaped me into being the best version of myself—still nothing close to the version that God had in mind when He created me though—it is obvious to me that for one to become aligned with their destiny they have to embrace the arduous journey that leads to their greatness. The fact that Jesus experienced agony beyond description—being mocked, being spat upon, being taunted by his enemies—and still to stay true to His nature, understanding the bigger picture, is one way to look at our pain. He was within His right to "appeal to Caesar" but He chose not to. Accepting rather the will of his Father, appealing to Him, He laid his life down.

For many years I was stuck in deep hatred and anger as I felt that I did not deserve the things that happened to me. I blamed everyone that had caused me pain without taking into account the ripple effects and my contributions to my own pain. I used to think that all men were out to get me. The fact that I was always either the only female—or one of two females on a team of ten plus men—felt like a curse. I was always ready to fight, even over who gets to speak first. It was not until I received professional help that I got to uncover the ugly truth about myself—that I was self-destructive without even being conscious about it. My therapist defines self-destructive behaviour as doing something that's sure to cause you harm—whether it's emotional or physical. Simply because I did not display the obvious signs of self-destructive behaviour—binge eating, impulsive and risky sexual behaviour, alcohol and drug abuse, self-injury—did not mean I was not guilty. I am a recovering shopaholic. For so long in my life I had assumed that being a shopaholic was sexy and a sign of financial freedom. Because I worked incredibly hard— sweating for every cent— I thought splashing myself with unplanned shopping sprees with my hard-earned cash was acceptable. "I deserve to be spoiled" I said—not knowing that I was actually filling a void. To go to Europe and back, to shop till you drop in a currency so much stronger than the Rand, appeared to be a sign of success to me. Until therapy I was notorious for being the last man standing. Cashiers knew my first name while store assistants made sure I had a wonderful time buying items I never needed nor wanted. I had joined the bandwagon that says shopping is a hobby. I really thank God that He sent me the most understanding man with high levels of emotional intelligence. If it was not for that, I would have been a divorcee by now, because I did my best to push him away. I was the most difficult person to deal with—let alone live with. He made concerted efforts to understand my childhood, my traumas and triggers, treating me like a queen even when I didn't deserve it. I had no room, no capacity to reciprocate the overwhelming love I was receiving from him, because I didn't love myself. It was only through my journey to self-discovery that I learned that I needed to love myself first, and from that place I would be able to truly love others—especially my husband. For the longest time I didn't know how to take in and accept his love—I viewed him as a love sick puppy.

He grew patient rather, instead of impatient. Instead of giving up on the dragon lady he taught me how to love myself and accept being loved. If that is not unconditional love, I don't know what is. For that reason, I say, Ree, not just one-of-a-kind, but... one-in-a-trillion.

28

Showing up

Degree under the belt and whatever else comes with it—expectations—I marched off with confidence into the future. All the world was mine, I knew, I had succeeded at last. Here was my piece of paper. You know it doesn't work that way but how was I to know? I had put all my faith in education and now? Education was going to put some faith in me.

We've been talking about temporary relief and how it is worse when the time comes for there to be no relief any more but back to surviving. I'd rather not have any relief, any windfall, any faith in anything that is not rock-solid. I'd been job hunting that year, and my previous work had ended. No steady income, no income at all. And the temptation was to take anything I could find—a campsite job. A teller at the bank, a call any more operator, anything to keep me going. I'd have volunteered for waving a flag at a construction site if it could pay my way. But something else said there is something better than that. And if you start along that road will you ever come back? You may as well travel back to where you started from. And settle down in the middle of nowhere. Choices... I think it has to do with faith. Faith-based decisions. *Without faith, you cannot please God.* So you step out. Even if it is only water you are stepping on. Or a long long road, not to freedom, no, but to Tyger Valley. For those of you who know Cape Town, you will know the mountain. No doubt the mountain has its place in the sun. But the valleys now, and the rivers, well… I know a little bit about them. So far no relief. No temporary relief. Struggling for survival, scraping for survival. But not so low that I would give up on that one thing that would justify my life up to now. If I was to work, I said, I would work where I wanted to. My view from the mountain top would be a view from the boardroom table. Looking down on the mountain. I'm telling you all about this because of the road it takes to get there. And the road you sometimes have to walk barefoot. I had my sights set on a position in an investment management firm. It was another side of the valley. My job was to get there on time. Upon this crossroads, I found myself Rand short for taxi fare to my interview. A Rand may not seem like a lot to you—and it isn't—but to me, at that moment it was the difference between…. well, having a future or not.

Ree had been saving up his pocket money every month to make sure we'd not be stranded when we were called for interviews. He too was looking for work—his allowance was all we had. Financial support for me had stopped with my qualification. I was expected to be out there I suppose and cracking it. Not walking the streets like an urchin. He would now and again lend people money— not a bad thing—it was one way we could guarantee cash flow when whoever it was returned the money. I had scheduled an interview for the coming Monday— he called his uncle to pay up and he was glad to oblige. "I'm hosting a braai this weekend," he said. "Bring your girlfriend." We sure did enjoy ourselves. It's not like we were having braais at our place every night. With us, it was more like whatever we could find to put into our three-legged pot. And what we could find to light a fire beneath it. In contrast, he spoiled us. If he intended to impress, we were impressed. A braai is a braai in any language, I don't care for barbecues. Something about South Africa—even if it is just boerewors—says a braai puts you on top. Just the meat itself. I'm not sure if you get anything else in the world like Karoo lamb. I'm sorry for the lamb but I'm grateful also. It was a lamb that was saved for the Passover and a lamb that was slain for our redemption. When I eat lamb chops at a braai I remember. Here was premium meat, expensive whiskey. The conversation flowed with the whiskey. While I have never been a drinker—for reasons you can appreciate—Ree had acquired the taste early, from his youth. "There's a difference between drinking for pleasure and drinking to get drunk," he says. But no mention of the money up to now. And as they say, money buys the whiskey. And the taxi trip. As we left the house he raised the issue and explained about my interview tomorrow. *"Awua ntate!"* (nigga please) he exclaimed. "What about all that meat you've just had?" It was a Laban moment for us. Do you know the devious uncle from Genesis in the Bible? So you thought you had put to bed the one daughter you loved—you who had served seven years for her—but wake up to find it's the one you don't like? And you must now work another seven years for the one you do?

"I don't!!!"

It's funny now but it was not funny then. He had decided all by himself to translate his debt to Ree as Ree's contribution to the braai. Only, like Laban with Jacob, without his knowledge or consent.

What???

We left while I was trying to gather my jaw from the floor. I'm no Rachel but really, Laban? With uncles like you, who needs family? Now the search started and the parable about the woman searching for her lost coin—only we did not find it—seek and seek as much as we like. "Seek and ye shall not find." From dining like kings and viewing things from the mountain top here we were again in the valley—under the bed if need be. Searching with our lamp under a bushel. Or under a mattress. It was way too late to be making calls, asking for help. To make things worse, I had to leave the house early in the morning—an awkward time to be calling around asking for money. It's never a good time to be asking anybody for anything but you know what it says: ask and it shall be given unto you.

Only I didn't ask for this.

But it was given to me anyway.

I decided to go ahead regardless, coins notwithstanding. I moved forward with hope, in blind faith, perhaps I'd stumble across a Rand—and not a stumbling block. I would even ask strangers for help—so long as it was not that uncle again. So, the money I had to get there, how was I to get back? I wonder how many people in life ever get to think this way. How many people have only ever had money to go one way but not money to get back? Who take the same step of blind faith and if it does not play out the way they hope they take the next step. So, this was my first round of the interview process. I arrived way ahead of time—never a good move. I've achieved most of what I needed to in my life in the last second or two. I went to the bathroom to freshen up and to look at myself in the mirror. I had to give myself a good talking to and remind the township girl that she was good enough and she's got this. There she looked back at me, the product of what? A township? Maybe.

Hardship? No doubt. Entrepreneurship? Let's see. Township girl? Career girl more like it. Successful girl? *Just look at you* I told her. *Just look at you* I told myself. *It's not like you didn't get yourself this far.* It was a dressing room moment. Camera, lights, action. *Don't worry girl. Don't worry about being up against experienced candidates. You've been here before and conquered.* Perhaps you don't believe in a God. Perhaps you don't believe in a devil. I only know one wanted me to be there and the other one didn't. *How are you planning to get back since you don't have enough money for the taxi fare?* You can tell me which one that was. My turn came and I was called in. I did not pretend to be something I was not but I was also not afraid to show what I was made of. And I wonder now if that is not the best way to go into an interview. Or through life for that matter. Now began my pilgrimage. My Great Trek. Some say the Voortrekkers passed over the mountains to get where they wanted to go. That they chose the most difficult route. Because that was in their nature. Me I just wanted to get to town so I could get to a bus and get out of here, back home. I had accomplished what I needed to, the interview had gone well. I wasn't looking for anything more than that, only to get home without it costing me. I thought maybe I would find a lift along the way. Maybe a neighbourly soul would help, a good Samaritan. But failing that I had my legs and my two feet. The only problem was my shoes. These were my interview shoes, not my walking shoes. They were not made for walking. This is the biggest lesson I learned about hope that no one told me before. Just because you are hoping for the best doesn't mean you are guaranteed the best. Hope is like fuel—its presence is meant to take you where you need to go—while its absence will get you stuck. I'm not quite sure how long that road was or how long it would be if I walked it again today. At the time it seemed like the long road to hell, let alone freedom. I'm sure you'd like to picture with me this corporate girl dressed up for the city walking the streets of nowhere. A lonely figure out of a painting with a distant horizon that never comes any closer.

I was no stranger to walking, but not like this. My feet were sore already, beginning to swell. My shoes were beginning to hurt. I kept on in the hope that in the next few minutes something would give. It carried on like that and it carried on, I kept telling myself over and over, *something will happen soon. It will all stop shortly. Just have faith.* But of course, it got to the point where I just could not walk any more. What was left of my shoes reflected well what was left of my hope— worn out and past repairing. By this time I must have covered half the distance. It's never a good thing to stop, I know that, nor to sit down.

To stop now, to take a seat… would I ever get back up again? Would I ever continue? But sit down I did and took my shoes off. There was nothing left of the heels. I don't know what stuff they make interview shoes from but it does not go together with life. Still, I could not give up. Still, I must hope. After all, what else was there? And what else was there still waiting for me? *"HAVE I NOT BEEN TORTURED ENOUGH IN LIFE?"* I hurled out into the universe. No, I had not. Apparently. I'm not sure if you can see the painting now with me sitting by the roadside with my head in my hands, my broken shoes dangling from my dangling wrists. If it was a name I could give the painting it would be Dejection. Which I suppose is the opposite of hope.

Add frustration.

Add disappointment.

Add affliction, yes.

Add crucifixion. *"FOR HOW MUCH LONGER? FOR HOW MUCH LONGER?"* the lonely figure in the painting screams at the clear blue sky. Part of me wanted to quit it all, but here's the thing, I had nothing to fall back on. And I had come such a long long way. "Oh Lord"—whoever he was—"oh god of hope… what hope is left for me?"

Carry on.

Carry on? Is that it? *It was not by making yourself heard, but by staying sane that you carried on the human heritage.* I had heard that before. Certainly, I had made myself heard, but what now?

Carry on.

So to carry on becomes your default option. At least that's what I was hearing. You have nothing to lose by trying over and over again. Having nothing to fall back on. I knew now what I had to do. There was nothing more to it. *Carry on.* Carry on I did, on bare feet. I wonder today still what I did with those shoes. They could make a painting all by themselves, Bare Feet I would call it, or Perseverance. And I'd hang it over the fireplace where I sit with Ree's expensive whiskey and think about Uncle Laban. When I got home I threw myself on Ree and wept my heart out. I can't tell you if I was weeping from the pain of blisters beneath my feet or from bare feet on a hot tar road or from blisters I endured as a child with no one to comfort me. I'd say the latter. But there I was dragging Ree into things he had no business in. I wanted him to comfort me for all those years of pain and suffering as a child. But where would he begin? How do you settle a debt that is not yours to begin with? Talk about triggers! You may say on one hand I was but that child again or you could ask how could I be so toxic and manipulative? Taking advantage of someone's love, tenderness, and sympathy like that? How was I different from a vulture? Ummm… I'm not the psychologist here. But this is the danger of not returning to the wounds of your past in order to find healing. Your ongoing pain puts you in the default position of wanting everyone you meet to pay for the sins of those that have hurt you in the past. It's the same with people as it is with countries, the same with countries as it is with people. We know what was done to us so we know what to do to others. Unless there is some other kind of god called forgiveness. The crazy thing is, this debt that you keep expecting to be settled has no maturity date. There is never a point where you get to feel that the debt has been paid in full for your pain. There is no amount of love that can quench the thirst of brokenness. That's how messed up I was. My brokenness had to be fixed from within. Here you can talk about one who came to take all our pain upon himself and pay the full price. There's no doubt the healing comes from within, from him. And maybe only he can do what no other man can do. Better to give than to receive they say but to receive is better when you need to receive. With all the love I was getting from Ree, I just couldn't receive it well, I had no idea how. I felt unworthy to be treated so gently—in my world I didn't deserve to be loved. Was there something wrong with him? I wonder now how often our relationships fail because we expect our partners to fill the void that only we can fill. If you have a broken person in a relationship, expect it to be either dysfunctional or one-sided. Mine was one-sided—I was a taker—a guilt-free taker. But the odd thing is, I was taking all the love and kindness but not receiving it. Needless to say, I was not reciprocating it either. After a couple of weeks I received a call back for the second round of interviews. This time we made sure there was more than enough money for the taxi fare—except I couldn't take a taxi. On the week of the interview we were house-sitting in the suburbs and taxis are a nightmare in the suburbs—I'd have to take a train. If you hear alarm bells ringing here you may well have taken a train trip once or twice in your life. If you hear more than alarm bells you have actually been in one for longer than an hour. Third Class. If you have spent the whole day there you will not want to enter a train ever again. Not in Cape Town anyway. My interview was scheduled for 12 noon as I remember. I left the house early enough to catch the train and boarding the train I paid scant attention to fellow passengers or engaging in casual chit chat. I had my head in my books again, in my future, rehearsing for my life. About an hour later I looked up to find myself in parts of Cape Town I had never seen before, dark and dismal and depressing parts—forgotten parts—forgotten by the world and by God. Then I knew what you already know… I had boarded the wrong train! I could have peed my pants on the spot. Only my CPU stopped me. Somehow I had to *knyp vas* (pinch tight) and maintain control. "Stay sane" as the man had said. Or find someone to tell you it was all one big April's fool joke, except we were in Augustish. Diep River said the signpost. Diep River. Deep Water. I tried thinking of a Bible verse at this point but all I could think of was a hymn. *"O come all ye faithful, joyful and triumphant..."* The strange spectre of my mother breaking into a hymn sent me into a panic. *No! Ree!* No doubt there is a valley of shadow and no doubt a river and no doubt there are waters this way and that way above your head but to hear a voice on the other side was like a lifeline being thrown out from a lifeboat. I'm not sure what kind of technology enables us to talk to each other the way we do—enabling us to maintain a link to humanity, to sanity—but on that day, in deep water, it was indeed my lifeline. And it's funny how in that situation, in that place, on that platform, here was just the man for the job. He knew the trains, the ins and outs, the system by which I could get myself out of there and back on the right track. What you needed to know about these trains were the numbers, not the names. The destinations were not painted in letters but in numerics—1234, 4321, etc—something I hadn't bothered myself with up to that point. The solution was to get off the train I was on and wait for the train that would take me back. Then from there, take the right train. Have you ever been in a place where you are as far from the place you want to be as heaven is from hell? And hell is this way and heaven is that way but you are in hell? That's what Diep River feels like when you are waiting for a train. Now, what to do. Apart from pacing furiously up and down. And blame Uncle Laban for his ongoing support. "Pray" you say. Pray. Yes, I will pray. For what? To turn back the hands of time? To stop the sun in the sky? And send it back two hours? And everything else too? At this point I was two hours late for my interview but somehow I still had to show up. If it was sheer willpower or sheer stubbornness or sheer stupidity or sheer obstinacy, I don't know. My step-father taught me well. With the situation out of my hands, I went back to my books. It was the only way to distract myself and detach myself from the situation. Again, it's handy having a partner in life. Handy to have someone to talk for you. Marriage is teamwork is all I know and here my partner stepped up again to make that call I could not make. A calm voice, focused, reassuring, comforting. "All would yet be well" the voice said. "She will be there" it said—and it was right. Five hours later I arrived. Five hours late for my interview. And looking like I hadn't showered in days. Looking like, well… like I had just walked through deep and darkest Africa. Tyger Valleys notwithstanding. And you know there are no tigers in Africa. Apart from the zoos, anyway. This time I got to meet the executive management. Fast forward, I went out of that interview no longer concerned whether I had bagged the job or not—the amount of support and compassion I received was adequate for me. As shrewd as they were said to be online when I was doing my research on the company, I saw a motherly side to them—women who embodied the true wisdom of knowing when to be an executive and when to be a mother. They were one-of-a-kind. I showed up, that was all that mattered. Or I was some kind of Very Important Person I did not know I was. There was no judgment on how I looked. I was welcomed with genuine warmth instead of the usual condescension. From there they offered me a glass of water and brought it right in front of me while I was still trying to catch my breath. They helped me to relax. They asked about my day from hell. We had a good laugh about it. They made me feel good. They put me at ease. I felt not only seen but heard. I was a human being—equal before man and God. I knew that was the company I wanted to work for because I could see I was not going to be just a number. They had waited how long for me—after working hours! I felt important, like I mattered. It made me realize that being important has always been my birthright, not a privilege—regardless of how I was raised to believe. By the time we started with the interview I had forgotten about the stains on my blouse and my hair that looked like I had just been raised from the dead. My shiny wet face, my sweaty body, were not even on my mind. Through creating a safe space for me, through encouraging me in this way, my confidence was restored. It was as if none of that nightmare stuff ever happened. At some point, I was asked when I was ready to start. *When I was ready to start??? What, with the rest of my life???* I was home. I returned one more time for a third-round interview with the

CEO and an offer I could not, would not, and did not refuse. Credit must be given here to the one man who joined that second-round interview—and was just as accommodating. If I didn't know better I'd say he had received a memo from Khulekani. From making sure I was familiar with the canteen system to practically training me for my job—sharing a few tricks and short cuts—he was never my appointed mentor and we were not even on the same team but the role he played in setting me up to succeed in my job was formidable. Put it this way, while my internship helped me to bridge the gap between theory and practice, he helped bridge the gap between my internship and the big boy's world.

"Why are you so nice to me Shaun?" I asked him one day.

"I'm investing in my future boss," he said, giggling. "On a serious note Asa, you're going to be your own boss one day and I want to keep my options open." Faith rewards faith and I wonder upon what point his investment in me will be my investment in him. It is often said that we can never see the picture through the scattered puzzle pieces. It was puzzling for me to be wearing my shoes out and remaining unemployed longer than I had anticipated. Among those scattered pieces I wasn't able to see the picture. My doubts, my weariness, my frustrations during those times only make sense in retrospect. They were not only testing my elasticity but my commitment to my vision, to my dreams. Things only made sense during my first two weeks when the CEO found me at the photocopy machine station trying to scan a letter I had written to my creditors. I was in debt way over my head for my studies and it would take years to pay back. He asked to see it and asked me how much. I told him. He said he'd pay it. I said what's the catch. No catch he said. But I could not believe it. There had to be something in it for him in the real world of real world transactions. This was no fairy tale ending or a Jesus walking the water moment. But you will find that too fits into the picture, that little puzzle piece.

A piece of debt that would have taken me ten years to pay off—debt I had incurred only to get myself out of slavery—to free myself from the devils of my past—was put in place as per one who was looking at the big picture. What kind of man was this I was thinking? What kind of angel? But really it was what kind of destiny. And what kind of shining light. Now I was happy that I missed out on all those other job opportunities that had seemed like what I needed. God had prepared something better, something greater! When it was all said and done, my crawling was not in vain. It was like I had to make an upfront deposit for my dreams through my scars—while God would take care of the balloon payment on my dreams. As per Abraham and Isaac, God would provide. "We have the wood" said Isaac to his father. "We have the fire. But where is the lamb?"

"God will provide a lamb, my son." Isn't it like that with every one of us? So I provided the fire, He provided the lamb, and here we are today, still alive. Isn't that what dreams are all about? A collaboration between us and God? God won't move until you move. Do the possible to prepare a way for God to do the impossible. That's what showing up is about. Was that my lucky break? I hardly think so. But I can't help but think of how things could have been had I not showed up for the interview when I took that wrong train.

The lesson? The beauty of doing your best and leaving the impossible to the Almighty. No one puts it better than Corrie Ten Boom, when she says "Never be afraid to trust an unknown future to a known God." Drawing from my life experiences and coaching career, I have observed that in our pursuit of personal growth, success, and fulfillment, we inevitably encounter countless challenges that test our limits. We find ourselves struggling to achieve seemingly unattainable goals while questioning the feasibility of our dreams. In moments like these, we are reminded of a fundamental truth that lies at the heart of our existence – the beauty of doing our best and leaving the impossible to God. Our journey through life is marked by milestones we set for ourselves – be it career ambitions, personal relationships, or spiritual goals. As we navigate through these milestones, we strive to reach our full potential by pushing ourselves beyond what we believe is possible. The beauty of doing our best lies in acknowledging our limitations while simultaneously recognizing our innate ability to rise above them. When we give our best effort, regardless of the outcome, we demonstrate an unwavering commitment towards self-improvement and growth. This dedication not only strengthens our character but also shapes it into resilience—a vital quality required to persevere through adversity. By focusing on what we can do rather than dwelling on what's out of our control, we cultivate a harmonious inner state that liberates us from the constraints imposed by incessant expectations. However, it's important to remember that even when we give it all, there may be circumstances that seem impossible to overcome. In such situations, acknowledging and accepting those limitations does not equate to failure; rather, it exemplifies wisdom. Surrendering these impossibilities to a higher power—be it God or any other entity you believe in—fosters faith in something beyond ourselves. Embracing faith can alleviate emotional burdens while instilling hope and optimism in us as we face obstacles in life. By placing trust in a divine entity and accepting its omniscience and omnipotence, we can let go of anxious self-doubt and insecurity—allowing us to immerse ourselves fully in the present moment. As we surrender to God and relinquish control, embracing vulnerability, we open ourselves up to the transformative power of faith that can lead us towards beauty and wisdom. The beauty of doing your best and leaving the impossible to God is multifaceted. It teaches you humility, resilience, and trust – virtues imperative in leading a fulfilling life. Moreover, it sows the seeds for a profound sense of gratitude as you learn to celebrate your accomplishments while also recognizing the divine intervention at play. Ultimately, our journey through life is one of self-discovery that leads us towards an understanding of our true capabilities and purpose. By committing ourselves to do our best and leaving the impossible to a higher power, we embrace an empowering philosophy that enables us to walk this path with grace and humility. In this state of harmony, we find genuine happiness, growth, and fulfillment as we blossom into our authentic selves—living with purpose and contentment. If I were to bring it home for the church folks, I'd say:

> *"I alone know the plans I have for you, plans to bring you prosperity and not disaster, plans to bring about the future you hope for. Then you will call to me. You will come and pray to me, and I will answer you. You will seek me, and you will find me because you will seek me with all your heart."* Jeremiah 29:11-13